From

Being

Kept *to*

Being Kept

Rochinda Pickens

Purpose Publishing
1503 Main Street #168 ♀ Grandview, Missouri
www.purposepublishing.com

Copyright © 2016 Rochinda Pickens

ISBN: 978-0-9979853-8-2

Editing by Felicia Murrell
Book Cover Design by PP Designers

All scripture contained in this book are referenced from the New King James Version, The Message, New Living Translation, Amplified and New International Versions of the Bible.

Printed in the United States of America.
First printing January 2017.
2nd Edition 2019

Dedication

To all my sisters around the world,

May you always look to God's Word to seek answers, find
solutions, and apply truth to every life circumstance and daily
living. I pray that you will have continued wisdom, knowledge,
and revelation of who HE IS and who YOU ARE as you search
the Bible, the Living Word where all accurate and infallible
teaching and instruction exist. It is the source of our true
identity and the Well of Life!

From Being Kept to Being Kept

Thank You

All the Glory and Praise to my Heavenly Father God who has been my source from the beginning and will be until to the end of time.

Special thanks to my husband Alan, who support and love is appreciated. To my children, Brittany, Darrell, and Andrea, your encouragement to do "ME" without holding back. To my Mom, Josephine Hooks, your amazing strength to persevere through it all. My family & friends who prayed and cheered me on in every facet of my life.

My baby sister Carlotta Berry, who proofed and read my drafts in the middle of the night and helped me recollect childhood memories. All of my siblings for allowing me to share our story with the masses.

Pastor Lia McIntosh my friend and sister in Christ, mentor and life Coach. Your leadership and teaching helped shape and develop me to be the best that God had created me to be. You gave me my first platform to teach and reach women through bible study.

My Best friend Rusha Morgan, you have supported me from the beginning, from elementary school until now; always cheering me on. Love you.

Lisa McLeod, my praying sister, who's always reminding me of God's unchanging and never ending love.

My Kept Women of God ladies, thank you for your commitment to go deeper with God. Thank you for allowing me to be the vessel to lead during our growth group bible studies.

Chinda's Boutique family, thank you for trusting me with your heart and your souls for the past eight years as we've connected while playing dress up.

My Renaissance church family, your love, support and needed prayers during this transitional season in my life has been amazing.

Thank you, Michelle Gines and Purpose Publishing for being there every step of the way. Your patience and expertise has been a blessing.

Foreword

In 2007, Rochinda and I met unexpectedly after the trauma of losing her husband, Darrell in a car crash. I was a student pastor at the church she attended and was called to provide support and counseling. She was broken, numb, and looking for direction. I was an inexperienced pastor who learned to simply be present and listen well through her journey. Little did we know God had much more in store for Rochinda and I. Four years later, in 2011, Rochinda and I partnered with a team to found Renaissance United Methodist Church and I had the honor of baptizing Andrea and Darrell. In 2014, Rochinda and Alan married and I had the privilege of officiating their wedding. Along the way, we have become more than pastor and church member. We have become sisters in spirit. I have witnessed Rochinda's renaissance as she journeyed from being kept by men to being kept by God. Today, she is a new woman in Christ.

This book shares the story of a strong, compassionate and gifted woman who dared to dream and work towards her life's purpose despite life's challenges. The choices Rochinda made were not always easy, but her faith propelled her to persevere. After losing Darrell, she could have easily retreated to the confines of a quiet widow's life. Instead, she chose to surrender and soar! In the past six years, Rochinda has led Bible Study groups, spent countless hours mentoring women, and launched a powerful "Kept Woman of God" (KWOG) ministry.

In this book, you'll find a resource to inspire you to courageous truth telling. There are few women that I know who would dare to tell their story as authentically as Rochinda has. It will also inspire you to answer the call of God for your life. Like Rochinda, we're all being called to experience renaissance. Renaissance is a renewal of life and vigor. It's a rebirth or revival. Importantly, you'll be reminded that you are not alone. In picking up this book you'll become a member of the KWOG community. It's a community of women who are unleashing our voices to bless the world through a deep relationship with God.

Prepare to be released from being kept by man to being kept by God!

Love and Blessings,

Lia

Rev. Lia McIntosh M. Div, MBA
Executive Coach & Seminar Leader

Table of Contents

Preface

Is this a dream or is this the real deal? Do I actually represent what a kept woman of God looks like, talks like? What about my style? Is it edgy? What about this blonde or when I'm really *feeling myself* platinum hair color? Do I understand the Bible well enough to share my life lessons?

I remember so clearly when I reached out for God's hand and He grasped mine and pulled me into His arms. The security I felt was overwhelming. I knew I would never ever let go again. Although I know this is real and it's no accident that you are reading my first book, it's still mind boggling to me and I'm sure to others as well. You see, I never envisioned myself as a writer because I simply felt like I had nothing important to say. If I did have something to say, I had no problem vocalizing my thoughts and feelings, but to put pen to paper, or should I say fingers to keyboard and, with vigor, share my revelation of what it truly means to be kept… It's quite surreal, humbling, and most of all, necessary.

As I sit upstairs in my makeshift office typing away on my brand new Asus laptop listening to the Isley Brothers on Pandora, the house is quite empty, except for my six year old standard poodle, Renni and I. From the day I brought him home, he's been my shadow. Where I go, he goes.

I still ask myself, "Is this really the life God has transitioned me into? Am I deserving of all these blessings that have been given to me?" Do you remember the song by J'LO? *It's Jennie on the Block*, or something like that. Well, my song will be titled *It's Rochinda from the Neighborhood Speaking Freedom*.

Who would have thought I would rise up and embrace the true meaning of being kept in the full realm of God? When I'm asked to speak or present for various functions, I sometimes wonder *is it me that you're requesting*? Just a few years earlier, I had never been asked to speak at a women's conference, although I had led several small groups along with facilitating several functions. But to be a part of sowing into the lives of women with spiritual guidance on how to live a life directed by God…

Are they really ready for me to break this subject all the way down? How will they receive the transparency I'm prepared to reveal? Will they be able to relate? Will they be able to see themselves in the stories I share with them, as I expose all the insecurities, hurts, wounds, and mistakes I made in an attempt to find security in a man? My prayer each time I share is that a soul will be healed as I speak truth about the pain and betrayal I once endured when I was blinded by the lies and deceit of men who mostly wanted only one thing.

I was asked to create a forty-five minute workshop for approximately one hundred ladies in two sessions, one morning and one afternoon. I responded instantly with a "yes," without any thought of what the workshop would consist of. Since the conference was called "This Love Thang," I knew God was ready for me to share what He had placed inside of me. I knew my story could no longer be a secret. I knew it was time every woman gain a clear precise understanding of what a kept woman versus a kept woman of God looked like, talked like, believed in, and put first in their lives. I needed to relinquish the falsehood behind what being kept meant.

As the women entered my workshop each were given two index cards and asked to briefly describe what they thought a kept woman was. I also asked them to define what a kept woman of God was. I received all kinds of misrepresentations of a kept woman spelled out on those small cards.

I noticed the expressions of deep thought on the women's faces while they wrote their definitions of being kept. Once complete, our discussion began with reading aloud their interesting, but not surprising, responses to the question of what a kept woman looked like. I wasn't surprised by what I heard because I too thought like that until the shift came into my life. The shift meaning, my surrender! What will your surrender be?

Many explained why they thought like they did and tried to justify their answers. I explained to them there was not a right or wrong answer. We all needed clarity so we could walk and stand in our God given purpose, not allowing the wrong strongholds to keep us captive.

My story on how I went *from being kept to being kept* will help you understand that when we are kept by the wrong things in life, it can take us to some "high places" that will eventually lead us into some very low and dark valleys. Yes, while we're experiencing the highs we lose sight of the truth. The title reflects bondage that has been released to a new profound freedom in God.

Are you ready to journey with me and get clarity on this kept business? If so, first write down what you think a kept woman is before going any further in this book. At the end of the book, ask yourself what or who is keeping me? Do you feel that your actions are being guided and led by God? Then reflect and ask yourself is there something keeping me that has stunted or stopped my growth from being kept by God. If so, are you ready and willing to do the work of surrendering it. Sometimes we simply get off track and need to be redirected. Unlike myself, I was totally lost and confused. I needed more than redirection, I needed a shift in the atmosphere to take place. I've had several in my life but none like this last shift that took place in Atlanta, GA, July 2010. As you continue to read, prayerfully your shift will take place as well.

Maybe your relationship has become stagnant and the intimacy you desire with the Lord seems out of reach. Ask yourself are you deserving of being kept by God? First thing, do you really want to experience the authentic benefits of allowing God to keep you? Speaking about myself, I never knew that all of this greatness even existed. What I'm saying is when we yield to the authority of God all other things should become secondary. At one time I was like many of you trying to fit God into my schedule after everything else was done. This meant God was often left out or given the short end of the stick. That was very wrong. How can we forget the Creator of the universe? The Creator who shaped and molded us and gave us life. If we go back to the beginning of time, *In the beginning God created the heaven and the earth* (Genesis 1:1). That means the universe. *God created man in his own image, in the image of God created he him; male and female created them* (Genesis 1:27). It's so clear to me now, but beforehand I was lost. We all are deserving of being a kept woman of God. Once we recognize and realize the desires of our heart are ready to be released, we can be, but only when we trust and believe the One who has given them to us. We must feel that we are deserving of all the love God has for us. God's love is unconditional and unchanging.

I was really confused about this kept woman and kept woman of God business. I didn't understand the correlation between the two. I had been studying for years how to be a kept woman by watching and listening to others. Only to find out that my teachers were broken students like myself or I only saw the surface of what I thought was good. We will never understand anything by grazing over the surface; we must study intently. I have finally entered into God's master plan for the duration of my time here on earth. His plan for my life cannot be glossed over or ignored. You cannot complete it overnight or put a time frame on the process. This is a lifestyle change that must be implemented in your daily routine. If you enter into the plan God has for your life, demonstrating obedience and complete trust, you will see and feel the cleansing of your heart and reshaping of your soul. How do I know this? Because you are reading my story *From Being Kept to Being Kept*. God's plan is the only plan that is unchanging, constant, and unwavering regardless of the ebbs and flows and the ups and downs we experience in life.

Do you think you can tell the difference between a kept woman versus a kept woman of God by her appearance? They both look the same from the outside with that clean polished look. Every strand of hair is in place, sporting the latest fashions and scented with the sweet smell of Chanel perfume. The handbag being carried is probably the latest inspired bag or one of the desired name brands. The lip color always applied with perfection and the jewelry intermingled with the real and the fake. Her entrance is always with confidence, shoulders broad, and her head held high. The car she drives is always consistently clean and anyone who sees her, always asks, "Who is that woman styling and profiling? I wonder who is keeping her." It's strange. I never heard the words kept woman of God until my life took a turn. That doesn't mean it didn't exist, it merely reveals I had blinders on and was clearly in the dark.

On the outside, both of these women look identical. But on the inside, one heart is being kept by God and the other is being kept by man. When we are kept by anything other than God, we allow ourselves to get caught up in bad situations. We even go as far as idolizing material things. When this happens we become enslaved by the source. Desperately wanting to maintain a particular lifestyle. And revenge and hurt are your driving forces to succeed. Deep rooted pain ready to be tilled. The doubt and fear is a constant reminder of being unworthy. The respect for yourself and others is evident in your actions. When we behave immorally or treat others wrongfully it's due to a lack of respect we have for ourselves. When you have self-respect no one can mess over you. Understand that you must embody who you are as a child of God, respecting who He is as your Lord and Savior. This will block all idols. Respect goes a very long way. Anything that is an idol over God will eventually lead you astray. An idol is any person or thing that is greatly admired, loved, or revered. When you know God is your keeper, you don't put anything before Him. You trust God and relinquish everything to Him and allow yourself to be kept in the realm of God where all things will work according to His plan for the goodness and perfect will of your life.

Chapter 1

How Do I Begin?

I was born October 4, 1964, to Charles Edward Berry and Josephine Ann Hooks in Kansas City, Missouri. I was sixth of seven children raised by a single mom. Actually, Mom was still married to my father but they separated when I was ten months old. I was a baby with no recollection of ever living with my father. However, when I got older, he told me stories about all of the fun things he did with my siblings and I. He would go into great detail about how I rode on his back as he pretended to be a horse. I seriously believed he had me mixed up with my older siblings since Mom left him when I was still a baby. Occasionally, I reminded him that I didn't remember. Most of the time, I allowed him to repeat his amusing stories without interruption since I didn't care to burst his bubble like I had done before. I'll never forget his handsome, red skin toned complexion becoming redder as he got excited. He would say, "Baby, I know what I'm talking about." From that time on, I decided there was no need to shatter his memory of what he recalled as opposed to what I remembered. Maybe I was the child in his descriptive, animated stories, maybe not. Nevertheless, I decided to allow Daddy to repeat his stories time and time again while I looked on and smiled and nodded, only recalling the experience from the last time he told me. I believe if he had the opportunity to go back in time and have a second chance to "get it right" as a husband to my mom and a father to his children, he would have.

Later in my adult life, while he battled courageously with lung cancer, I developed a closer relationship with my father. Our relationship evolved into more of a friendship, and I felt more comfortable asking him some tough questions. I felt it was the proper time to seek answers and that I was ready to receive his truthful responses without being angry about the *why*. The daddy that was generally lighthearted and easy going in the way he spoke became serious and melancholy as he attempted to provide answers to my much needed questions. His responses didn't erase the many years of neglect I felt while he was absent from my life, but I better understood some of the decisions he made, even the ones he didn't make. The one on one, eye opening conversations may not have happened if he hadn't become sick. I took great care of him while he battled lung cancer, taking him to many of his doctor appointments since I was the one child living in Kansas City that was available during the day. Our mom let us develop our own opinion about our dad. Once we got older, she spoke more bluntly about him. And, sometimes it was a little bit too much. He was still my daddy and I loved him. Her experience with him was just that, her experience. But Mom didn't have to tell us what he did or didn't do. As I got older, I was able to draw my own conclusions and piece them together by what my daddy didn't say. Regardless of what I remember or recalled as a young child, Dad's recollection of what he did "Kept" a smile on his face as he shared with countless people. We can tell a story over and over and sometimes it gets embedded in us that it's the truth. I told myself over and over that I was happy, healthy and whole. I too was being kept by LIES, deep hurt buried inside of me.

My father was known as Good Time Charlie. It is very important that you envision what my father looked and acted like. These same characteristics are what I longed and searched for. He was a distinguished good looking man, quite charming. He stood 6'1" and weighed approximately 185 pounds. He was always well-groomed and dressed to impress. Daddy was charismatic and funny. He was a real sweet gentleman. No one was a stranger to him, and he loved women. Daddy didn't discriminate when it came to women, especially if they could cook, clean, and, of course, treat him like a king. And, the women I met loved my daddy. Now, they had to have good personal hygiene, smell of perfume, and daddy preferred long hair. Daddy loved long hair. But for the most part, he had no certain type of woman when it came to their body type, facial features, or their career choice. However, one key attribute that was non-negotiable was she had to know how to cook. Daddy indulged in drinking and partying and simply having a good ole time. It was often that you'd see him with a cigarette dangling from his lips or propped skillfully between his long, thick index and middle finger in preparation to take another draw of the dangerous smoke that would eventually take my daddy away from me for good.

Many years before his fate, Daddy did quit due to a scare when he went in for a chest x-ray. He put the cigarettes down cold turkey, and I never saw him take another puff. It was music to my ears to hear him later complain of the smelly stench when in the space of others that smoked. I couldn't be more proud of him. Now, I'm not sure if I ever told him, but I'm sure he knew since he knew how much I hated him smoking. Twenty some years later after quitting, he was diagnosed with lung cancer and a few years ago, Daddy succumbed to the ugly disease. Daddy also had a love affair with food and friends were considered family, which was part of the strain on his marriage with my mother.

All who knew my daddy loved him immensely and never spoke anything bad against him. Let Mama tell it and she'd say, "It was hard enough feeding seven kids and, your father, let alone all the "friends" that were invited to eat and hang out at our home. What was he thinking? Bringing all these strangers into the home unannounced." I guess he wasn't thinking about the consequences that would later take place. He loved his blue bib overalls, lightly starched with a well defined crease. He always sported his Stetson hat and Stacy Adam shoes, wearing a scent of Old Spice cologne which always filled the room. You could smell it miles away. Still to this day, when I smell the scent it is a constant reminder of the man who I loved with all my heart. He transitioned to heaven on December 30, 2014.

Mom, known as Candy back in their days, was fine as wine. She stood 5'7" tall, weighing 120 pounds. She changed her hair as often as most people changed their underwear, from wigs, cornrows to short afros. She was often seen sporting her hoop earrings. Since I was good at French braiding, I had to braid Mom's hair at least twice a month. I didn't mind doing it when there wasn't anything else to do, but it seemed she preferred Friday evening when I was looking forward to hanging outside with friends. And if you knew my mom when she tells you she needs her hair braided, all you can say is, "Yes ma'am." Mom kind of favored Diahann Carroll and Cleopatra Jones all rolled into one depending on the day.

Like Dad, she loved to dance. As a kid, I imagined her Estée Lauder fragrance which smelled like heaven, was like her magic potion that made her dance with such rhythm. At Christmas time, she always got that cute little set with the bow attached on the outside of the bottle. As a little girl, I would sneak into her wide collection of perfumes accumulated over birthdays, Christmases, Mothers Day's, Valentine Days or just because days. My mom loved to dance the night away and have a good time. Like Daddy, she was also a smoker who gave up smoking too, but much earlier than Daddy did. Looking back, I see how mom gradually eliminated bad habits out of her lifestyle in effort to live a better life. I remember the day vividly. She sent my baby sister Carlotta and me to the neighborhood grocery store to buy her two cartons of cigarettes. She said after they were gone, she was done. And just like that, we never saw her smoke another cigarette. I always thought she made smoking look sophisticated, so it took a minute to get accustomed to not seeing her take in the sounds of Marvin Gaye, Diana Ross, or some other hit album spinning on the turntable of her brown and black record player while she sat in her favorite crush velvet blue chair on a Friday night puffing away. I never picked up the bad habit, but several of my siblings started their nicotine love affair at very young ages.

24

I'm guessing it's because my parents were heavy smokers.

When Mom met our father she already had two children from a previous marriage and relationship. At the age of fourteen, Mom gave birth to her first child Marilyn, whom we called by her middle name Rene. She had my brother Joe at fifteen. Dad came on the scene when Mom was around seventeen. They married and conceived five children together - Marsha, Delano, Tina, Carlotta and me. My mom birthed seven children by the time she was twenty-four years old. Having seven children boggles my mind, even at my age now, let alone the idea of barely being a teenager when she started motherhood and continuing to give birth up until she finely wised up. The story goes that Grandma warned mama about daddy and her having all these babies. She wanted better for her daughter and Grandma was certain that mom being 'knocked up' on a continual basis wasn't going to lead her down a successful road.

The average lady with seven mouths to feed would have surely lost their mind, but not my mother. I'm sure she fell into a panic from time to time when the money came up short and she had no clue how to make ends meet. Who would blame her if she felt her life was doomed with limited resources and restrictions with seven mouths to feed. But Mama was strong, not only in physical strength, mentally and emotionally too. Her determination would not allow for a pity party. She knew the only way was up and out of a life of poverty. Yes, poverty. We were poor like everyone else, but with Mom's mentality of fake it until you make it, and being a private person, not many knew her daily struggle. She wanted to lead by example and prove to herself and everyone else who counted her out that she would make a better life for her family. We were more than our surroundings and the example of being kept by God was evident back then as well as now.

Dad was employed with Sawyers Trucking Company and Mom was a nurse's aide at night. She was home with me and my siblings during the day when school wasn't in. With barely a high school education and limited funds, Mom's frustration was hidden from all. Except for us, we knew the real deal. With a house full of babies and Dad's ongoing partying and drinking, money was spent when it should have been saved or used on the family. Dad's coming in and out of the house at late hours finally ran its course with Mom. Sure, she joined in on the "fun" from time to time, but enough was enough. Their hot, steamy relationship finally turned into a cold and weary one. Mama knew she needed to make a change for her children. One thing about my mom, when she says she's done then she is DONE! The road that she was on had been keeping her immobile. What I admire about my mom is that she instilled great strength and determination in me. Right or wrong, she always told me to never give up and be able to take care of myself at all times. Our mom demonstrated great strength when she decided to walk by faith not by sight (2 Corinthians 5:7). She made a change in her life that affected seven children not knowing what the outcome would be, trusting and believing that the change would be better for all without having a blueprint or instructions on what and how.

I don't remember, because I was so young, but I've heard the story about how she loaded us up in the family station wagon and off we went to live with Grandma Hooks and our step grandfather Gus Kerr, my mom's mother and stepdad. Grandma Hooks was petite in stature. She was particular about everything in her home. We respected her home and stayed in our designated area. Remember, our mom left home at an early age, so she wasn't thrilled about returning with all of us. You can only imagine what was going on in her head upon returning to her mother who had been disappointed by her initial departure at fourteen years of age. Like most typical, rebellious teenagers that age, she believed she knew everything and had the misconception that she was grown. Just a side note: Never burn bridges you may have to cross later.

Mom was the only girl surrounded by her four brothers and raised by a single mother. She was the middle child. I'm guessing her toughness came from being raised with all boys. She told us Grandma would fuss about her cutting her hair. Perhaps because she was the only girl, Grandma wanted her daughter to at least look like one.

We made our temporary home on the third floor of Grandma's house. Mom's heart wanted to give Daddy chances to make their marriage work, but she knew in her mind the results would be the same. As I said before she was done. Carlotta and I were babies. Therefore, we relied on our older siblings to us in on the details of life at Grandma's house. When we did get a little older, our life quickly adjusted to what we were used to. Life without our father was the norm for us. There were occasional visits from Dad, but they were often brief and never consistent. We lived with our Grandma for quite a while until she purchased a new home. Grandma wanted a smaller home for herself and Grandpa Gus, turning her old home over to Mom and us. Mom was elated about having the opportunity to have a home of her own but still it wasn't the house she had chosen on her own accord. That would have to wait at least for now. There was something about being independent that made a huge difference for Mom. Our mom was a nurse's aide at St. Joseph Hospital and was also enrolled in a program to help her get back on track. Mom was being kept by her own thoughts of proving herself once again to all.

Many of us have been kept by something but haven't quite figured out what that is. At the end of each chapter I have created a few questions that I had to ask myself before moving forward. As you read this book in its' entirety, ask yourself this:

"If I start from the beginning - what will I uncover?"

Chapter 1

Q:

Where do you begin?

A:

No matter what you are dealing with, you must get to the root. Although the roots may be mingled, old and tattered we still must start from the beginning.

NOW LET'S WRITE
YOUR ANSWERS

_____
_____
_____
_____
_____
_____
_____
_____
_____
_____
_____
_____
_____
_____
_____
_____
_____
_____
_____
_____
_____
_____
_____
_____

Chapter 2

Memories

How far back can you remember? Or should I say how far back do you want to remember? Is your memory clear and precise? Does your childhood memories play an important part in your life today? Remembering my past was a healing process for me, the hidden and covered up scars had been bandaged up for quite some time that they appeared to be healed. Therefore, the bare eye would not have noticed the scars of my past. Most of the time, it's hard to uncover the truth about ourselves when we are in denial. Well, let me rephrase this. For me, being able to admit the truth was recognizing my brokenness. In order to be healed and set free, I had to snatch off all the bandages bit by bit and tackle each infected area. Was it easy? Absolutely not. The hardest part was actually revisiting my past. There were things in there I wanted to keep dormant, but I knew it wasn't up to me. There was some stuff from my past that contributed to my behavior as an adult. Not all, but a vast majority. A

31

simple tone in my mom's voice shaped how I would talk to my own children. The authority over our household impacted how I ran my own. It was normal for me to see a woman in charge of everything. The hugs I never received caused me to desire and give inappropriate affection. The insistent nightly prayers by my sister shaped me to believe she could handle it all. The closeness I had with my sisters taught me to value sisterhood. The arrogant remarks made by my oldest brother were a constant reminder of self-demeaning and superiority. The rigorous play and constant teasing caused me to avoid interaction. The good, bad, innocent and the ugly will shape you and put you on a road of no return when you are lost and confused and trying to find your way. Let's begin examining "From being kept."

Around the age of eight, we moved to our first home. Mom was qualified to purchase based on a program she participated in. This program was developed to help young mothers get back on their feet. Part of the requirements were, she had to maintain employment and be enrolled in an educational program. This meant long days for Mama -- work during the day and school in the evening. This is a great example of my mom's ability to go from being kept by the government system to being kept by her own willpower to succeed. I can't recall everything that took place during our move, but my older siblings said everyone was looking forward to it.

All we knew when we left Grandma's house, was that we were moving and we would finally have a home of our own. That meant bigger bedrooms and no more having to be quiet as Grandma slept; it's our house now. Mom's financial status and lack of education put her in a place of restrictions. A place that controlled where and when she could move in life. It also controlled how much time she was able to spend with her children and her ability to maintain a healthy balance in life. Simply put, our grandparents' ability to take us in allowed mom to embark on a new life of stability and save money to move forward.

From what I was told, Mom appeared to be getting her footing back. Her behavior shifted to pride. I believe she was slowly getting her life on track, being able to see her name on the deed of her home was a sense of accomplishment. Mom was my first example of how to trust God in believing for His perfect timing and provision. *Wait on the Lord; be of good courage, and he shall strength thine heart: wait, I say on the Lord* (Psalms 27:14). Of course, I didn't realize God had everything to do with our move. I assumed it was all mom's doing. Our mom was all we had and was our example of strength. I was too young to understand anything and really didn't care to know. *"From Being Kept"* is a reminder of something missing, absent or taken away. From being kept had some deep roots; roots that took on the shape of brokenness, loneliness, fear, anger and hopelessness.

33

What I didn't realize was these roots had stunted the growth of many including my parents. I was in survival mode and in training to do life the best I saw before me. Being trained up on how to be kept without missing a beat. I believed I had the best teacher for the job, my mom and dad. My training came from inside and outside of our home. Even when it wasn't the most ideal I followed, it appeared to be working for everyone else. What I learned help me navigate through life even with all the bumps and bruises. Mom was trying to get a handle on this new life, therefore the rules she put in place and the chores that were demanded of us was simply an example of who was in charge and who paid the bills. I did what I was told because it was demanded of me. Another example of being kept. Mom took care of us, she kept us busy! See, you may think that because you are busy, it will fix whatever issues you may be dealing with. Like Mom, she tried to keep us busy but still the busyness didn't replace what was missing. What was missing? I was missing the attention of my father and quality time with mom. My foundation was built on a sinking structure. A structure that one day would give way. When our foundation is structured on sand, when the water flows in at a consistent rate eventually we will have to rebuild. It's never too late to rebuild, start over and get it right.

Chapter 2

Q:

Are your memories the truth or lies?

A:

Memories could be either, depends on who is recollecting the memories. Are you ready to remember those painful memories and quit covering them up? What about trying to convince yourself that those painful memories are gone and weren't important?

NOW LET'S WRITE
YOUR ANSWERS

_____
_____
_____
_____
_____
_____
_____
_____
_____
_____
_____
_____
_____
_____
_____
_____
_____
_____
_____
_____
_____
_____

Chapter 3

Perception

I had a very broad imagination and was always so creative with my thinking. Alongside my baby sister, it was never unusual to find us playing or creating something new with cardboard boxes or creating dessert with bread, sugar and a dash of cinnamon. Sometimes we acted like we were on a road trip and imagined ourselves driving far away to an imaginary castle. I would change my voice and act like I was the good witch and reward her with lots of gifts. I went as far as being very descriptive about each gift. Sometimes Carlotta would blurt out it wasn't what she wanted or what she asked for. I would tell her she was spoiling the fun and to play along and stop whining. I loved turning cartwheels up and down the sidewalk when I was allowed to go outside. I craved my mom's attention hoping she would watch me while she sat on the front porch listening to her music. There were times I could see her lift up from her seat to look, but she never complimented me on how great I was with mastering the difficult flip it took months for me to learn. Years later, she shared with me how amazed she was at how high I could jump with such determination and agility. It sure would have been nice to hear some of those compliments then. I remembered being told to sit my fast butt down and stop all that flipping before I bust my head. I wasn't doing anything harmful, just trying to occupy myself and do what little girls do. A little attention from mom wouldn't hurt either. I always wore shorts underneath my dress so I was prepared at all times. Every chance I got, I flipped anyway. Our neighborhood was full of children, but we were told we didn't need to have any company at our house because there was enough of us as it was. We understood, but it didn't change the fact that we grew tired of each other and wanted to extend our play time to friends outside of our home. Eventually Mom allowed us to have company in front of the house, but never inside. I realized later in life it is best not to have people running in and out of your home. If something came up missing, it was certain that it was an inside job. As I played dress up, I imagined being a top model and I'd prance around the house with a book on my head in an attempt to walk as gracefully as the top models did back in my day. I was super skinny and I loved Beverly Johnson, watching her on TV or on the cover of the magazines I saw at the grocery store. I was very shy in public, but amongst my family and in my own element, I would shine and be so creative. Although we were limited on resources, nothing limited my mind from dreaming big about walking the runway one day. We sang and danced and played house. I played mama and Carlotta was the daddy. All we had was each other along with our make believe stories. Carlotta was always playing like she was a preacher praying for the dead bugs that we killed ourselves and then performed a make believe funeral. We actually made ourselves cry real tears. I should have known back then we had an anointing on our lives. We had convinced ourselves that one day we both would be famous and always promised each other that no matter what we would be each other's keeper, through thick and thin, rich and poor.

I spent a lot of time creating in my mind the fabulous life of being treated well and cared for like a queen. All the ladies I had seen didn't appear any better than me so I knew it could be done. I always admired and became mesmerized by the beautiful well kept women I encountered in the stores. I would sneak and wave at them and always give them a smile. I was amazed by their style of clothing and how poised they were. All were so well put together and it appeared they had pretty much what they wanted and needed. As a child, I didn't know exactly what these ladies did for a living. All I saw was what was projected on the outside. I was a very young girl with an impressionable mind. A mind that had already started taking shape to what I had seen and heard. Even the ladies I saw at church always looked well put together. The strangest thing was I didn't see the presence of many men. The men I saw most were the church deacons or the men that were seen after hours in the neighborhood. A few of the families that had men around were mostly drunks or abusive to the women. Mom would send us off to church for Sunday school and would show up sometimes for church service. She never told us if she was coming or not, but we knew we better be at church when she arrived. After Sunday school, sometimes we would use our offering money to buy candy at the house across the street that was actually a makeshift candy store in the front living room. I don't remember being told the purpose of giving our offering. I just knew we were supposed to give up our two quarters every Sunday. When Mom arrived, she too was always dressed nice not showing the daily struggle she endured and what it took for her to be at church.

One of our friends was mighty persistent in making sure we were up and ready every Sunday. She would call us the night before and remind us that we had church the next day. She was an only child, beautiful and well dressed. Her fingernails were always painted pretty. We thought she had it made because she lived with both of her parents and was spoiled rotten. Every Sunday, she walked up the street and knocked on our door to see if we would be attending church. Eventually, we started hiding from her because we respected and valued her opinion. We didn't want her to know that most Sundays we preferred to stay home. She was the Bible scholar in our neighborhood, always quoting scriptures and couldn't fathom why one would want to miss church. I guess her parents must have studied the Bible with her or somebody had. I never told her I'd rather sit and watch the neighborhood ladies sneak around with other peoples' husbands or boyfriends. It was like watching a drive in movie with three or four different screens: love story, drama, western and comedy. Of course I was sold on the love story that I thought would end happily ever after. From where I sat, it always looked like a happy ending. The damsel in distress always got the white knight. At that time, I didn't know the damsel was being abused by the so called white knight. I later realized most of the women who had night callers were in relationships with other men or they were married, but separated. These men represented the white knight I had dreamed about. However, because they were married, they were a distorted version of that dream. I always wondered how these single women afforded the things they had. Remember most of our neighbors were on government assistance and worked part time jobs. They had a house full of children like us, though maybe not as many. Where were the fathers? I knew where mine was and his absence chipped away at me daily. Why weren't their dads around? I wasn't sure why mine wasn't. Surely the blame wasn't on all of the mothers that were left behind. I don't remember anyone in the neighborhood's father ever dying. If so, it would have been understandable why their mom was alone. A few families were husband and wife, but mostly single women made up our community. What stood out most for me was these women were all holding down their families without missing a beat. They all displayed the strength of a woman. They made it look easy and the appearance of bling was always beaming when they stepped out on the town. I would sit and watch the lady from across the way. She drove a nice car and she dated a very young guy. In fact, she had several boyfriends, an old guy and a younger one. The younger gentleman was incredibly handsome, but she was twice his age. They would go out and come back arguing. He always beat her up and the police were called. After the police left, we would see her in her bra kissing and making out with him on her glassed in porch until the next incident arose. As my brain wandered, I imagined being able to have everything my heart desired -- clothes, a home, money, but not all of the fighting. I thought it would be nice to be on the arm of a very good looking guy from time to time. If a man ever thought about putting his hand on me though, he would soon find out I wasn't the one. Mom had taught us to pick up something and beat the crap out of a person if necessary. However, she reminded us if we ever hit first, we should expect to get hit back. She was serious about that too. I never put my hand on anyone out of fear of being hit back. I was definitely not a fighter we'll leave that with my baby sister Carlotta, who fought many of my childhood battles.

I knew Mom was no joke. I learned early not to get her involved unless it was serious. Thinking back, I remember a time when I was catching the city bus to work, which was my first job at the Internal Revenue Service located on Bannister Road and Troost Avenue. Since I took the same route every day, my pattern never changed. Like clockwork, I noticed a white man following me. I didn't know what he was up to, but I knew it was something strange which made me uneasy. I didn't want to go to work so my mom handled it. For a whole week, she would show up on her lunch break until I got on the bus safely. It was something about knowing Mom was there when I needed her most. The reason I shared that experience is because this is how I now feel about God. It is something about knowing God has my back at all times, even when I'm lost. Not comparing Mom to God, but she did whatever she had to to assure our safety as long as we told her what the problem was. The difference is, we don't have to tell God our problems. He already knows them. We only need to trust and believe God is able. All I needed was the attention of my parents, knowing they would always be there for me no matter what.

As children, we sometimes think our parents are mind readers and think they should always know what is going on. But the truth is, if your parent was like mine, they may not have had the time or energy to deal with much. Mom was a very young, single mother that had to choose between nurturing her children and feeding them. I'm grateful she chose to feed us, I would have hated to go hungry. Thinking back I realize it wasn't that my mom didn't have an interest in what I was doing, she was responsible for seven of us. Who was *Keeping* her during all of this? I never gave much thought to how she was feeling or what obstacles she was dealing with each day. Mom, thank you for wanting more for your children and choosing to move forward in your life.

Chapter 3

Q:

Define the word Perception?

A:

A belief or opinion, often held by many people and based on how things appear.

Do you believe your perception of your past has any effects on your presence? Is it possible that your perception could have been the catalyst of self-destruction?

NOW LET'S WRITE
YOUR ANSWERS

_____

_____

_____

_____

_____

_____

_____

_____

_____

_____

_____

_____

_____

_____

_____

_____

_____

_____

_____

_____

_____

_____

_____

_____

Rejection

One rainy fall afternoon, my sister and I were sitting on the front porch. We saw a man go over to our neighbor's house. This man resembled our father, but we couldn't get a clear view as he walked between the trees. He walked liked our dad and the car looked exactly like his. We tried to peek through the screened in porch without being noticed, but the view was distorted. With the houses sitting so closely in proximity, we could see the shadow of our neighbors scurrying to the door to let the gentleman caller in and we could no longer see the view. All we heard was the squeaky voice of the woman saying "I miss you" and "I've been waiting". The door closed behind them and we convinced ourselves it wasn't him and continued doing whatever mischief we were into at that given time. There was no way he would visit the single lady next door who had everything including her own child and not pay us a visit, of course not. Our father had other children by a previous marriage and another relationship. If my count is accurate, Dad had a total of twelve children. Two were stepchildren and our neighbor's child wasn't one of them. Two of the children came along while he was married to Mom, but we didn't find that out until years later.

It was strange to see my mom and dad interact. Sometimes he appeared to be flirting with Mom even while she fussed at him about what we needed. Carlotta and I would have our ear up against the vent listening to their conversation. Most of the time, the conversation was so muffled we couldn't always make out what was being said. Once, I heard him say, "You will always be my wife." Although Mom was separated, she was still married to our father. If Dad felt that Mom would always be his wife, why didn't he choose to be a better husband and father?

A few weeks passed and we eventually made friends with our wonderful neighbor only to discover our father was indeed hanging out next door. I was completely crushed inside, but we thought perhaps we would get to see him more since he was hanging out over there. Even though Dad didn't live far from us, his place was only big enough for him. Mom always said if he wanted us to come and stay or visit, he would have had a bigger place. That was her way of saying he don't want y'all living with him. We really didn't care. All we wanted was his attention, love and time. The little neighbor girl called our dad, *Uncle*.

48

She said he was her mom's boyfriend. This really pissed me off. I told her she was a liar and that she was going to go to hell for lying. I made her cry and she ran in the house and told her mom what I said. After that, she wasn't allowed to play with us for a while. We didn't care one way or another. We only wanted to keep tabs on our father. Our dad would pick them up every weekend take them to the swap and shop and the drive in movie. We were always left behind. Sometimes, he would even take our neighbor's relatives along with them. One Saturday evening, we noticed Dad and his girlfriend, along with her friends and relatives, were all dressed up. They were going to a Bobby Blue Bland concert. We knew all of the details because our dad's girlfriend's chatty daughter told everything not realizing what it was doing to us. They all left their cars parked out front in the neighborhood. Dad's girlfriend had a sister that was arrogant and hateful. Apparently one day our dog King got off his leash and chased after her causing her to kick him. My crazy brother Joe witnessed this and decided one day he would get her back for kicking our dog. So the night of the concert, he put sugar in her gas tank, which damaged the engine. We watched the next morning as they towed her car away and never said a word. As a family, we always stuck together to the end, right or wrong.

During all the mishaps in my life, I still continued to wonder about what I was seeing between my dad and our neighbor. I was confused. How could one be married with children and manage to have a relationship in broad daylight and provide for others before their own? Wasn't there a written rule somewhere that this was inappropriate? What about your morals? What was the definition of marriage? My beliefs were marriage was between one man and one woman that are committed to one another. My dad had several women therefore the commitment was gone. What about *till death do you part*? Since neither of them had died, it seemed to me they should have been working on their marriage. I believe my parents forgot about their vows and commitment to us as a family. I don't know how much my Dad was supporting his girlfriend and her daughter, but I knew we were doing without because I had very little of everything. My clothes were either too small or worn out, until we got new clothes for school and if Mom had any extra money, we got new outfits for Christmas and Independence Day. Grandma bought our underclothes and socks. Those were the things we needed most. We were taught, regardless of what you had, there was no reason to be dirty and our clothing should be clean as long as there was soap and water. You could always hand wash if you had to. When I went to school, even though I wore the same thing over and over, I took pride in being clean and neat. My heart was hurting as I tried to act like nothing was wrong. I always felt like a misfit. I was a ticking time bomb waiting to explode, but I didn't know it. I began to feel rejected and went into my own little cocoon without expressing to anyone what I felt. Getting dress for school was always a nightmare, trying to piece something together.

As much time as I spent playing with my younger sister, we never discussed how or what we were feeling. We just watched, absorbed and reacted. My childhood dreams quietly diminished. I grew up and developed my own identity and ideas about what was actually taking place. I started looking at men a little bit differently. The role of a man that should've been respected had taken a back seat to everything else. I had watched my mom early on conquer a bunch of STUFF. I started questioning if we had done something wrong as a family or maybe Dad didn't really want any more children. Since Mom did leave when I was ten months old, perhaps they argued about me. That couldn't have been it because, ten months later, they had another child. What happened to cause our family to split? My parents both had a different story on what happened. As I got older I realized it had nothing to do with me. Their issues were beyond me. I'm pretty sure my parents didn't map out ways to destroy their marriage or our family. And I know my mom's goals were not to be a single mom of seven struggling day after day. Why did Dad stop caring for us? It probably isn't fair to say he totally stopped caring for us. Instead, I'll say why didn't our Dad put his family first? I know he had to love Mom since he made her his wife and they conceived five children together. What did we do to deserve being mistreated? I guess mistreated could be a little harsh, but that's how I felt. I didn't appreciate having to share my dad with everyone else. Was I selfish? I don't think so. I was in desperate need of a father to demonstrate love, strength, security, trust and much more. To answer my own question, I had done absolutely nothing to deserve the rejection I felt. We had no say in this matter. Our parents made this decision on their own. Our family was truly affected by the separation of our parents. Everyone felt the hurt and rejection that was placed on us, but we went about life like nothing had happened, holding everything in as though we had a healthy happy family. Don't misunderstand. I was a physically healthy and a happy child, but there was an emotional disconnect and a deep loss that needed to be found. I remember always watching the cars in the neighborhood in hopes of seeing my dad's station wagon pass by. Sometimes thinking maybe he would stop and visit his girlfriend today and just maybe I would catch a glimpse.

Our neighbors had no idea what they were doing to innocent children that had been watching. I've always told my children that you never know who is watching you. You can either help the situation or make it worse. Which do you choose to do? The choices you make now will later impact someone's life good or bad. My dad and his girlfriend had no idea what we thought and they probably didn't care at the time. I remember some of their conversations clearly because of the closeness of our houses. The loud music being played while they entertained each other as I listened from afar. Although she looked completely happy and wanted for nothing, she may have been dealing with rejection herself. What other possible reason would you date a married man? I can come up with several; insecure, lack of self-esteem and totally lost. It didn't matter if he was separated, he was still married. I was so furious at times because they had something I wanted. That's all that mattered to me. Every time I saw them with shopping bags, it was a reminder of what I needed and didn't have. Even when our neighbors spoke highly of him, it was a reminder that they had his attention. I sometimes wonder if they intentionally rubbed it in our faces that they had our dad all to themselves. We will never know the truth. I eventually told my mom, but she didn't appear to be bothered by it at all. If she was, she covered it well. Her expression said good riddance but, I can only assume her heart held hurt and rejection. Mom tried desperately hard not to talk badly about our father. At times, I would ask mom if she thought the marriage could be saved. Her response was always the same, "NO." We only heard her arguing about money when he made promises that he didn't keep. Most of the time, the promises pertained to something we needed. He failed short on a regular basis. I never understood why we didn't receive child support. I'm sure there is a story behind that madness. I heard that every time child support was initiated, my dad changed jobs. If he changed jobs on purpose to keep from paying child support that was a poor mindset. Now days, you would be put in jail if you don't pay your child support. All of my dad's actions demonstrated being kept by popularity of life. It may sound strange, but my dad loved the attention of everyone and was very much a pleaser to any and everybody. When he saw us, he appeared to be satisfied with the brief encounters because I never heard him complain about visiting a little longer. There were no visitation rights in place because there was no court order. Being a family man was not a popular choice for him. Dad's track record showed the street life was more fulfilling to him. Yes, he did love all of us because we were a part of him and he always bragged about how many children he had and how all of us were good looking, especially the girls. No offense to our brothers.

After living in my own daytime soap opera, I came up with my own solution. I decided when I grew up, I was going to allow someone to take care of me. I was going to benefit like everyone else had been by being a *kept woman*. I had witnessed the perks and the treasures that were received. I saw what money could buy and without it one's life would lack much. I knew whatever my heart desired I was going to be intentional about making it happen. I had a dysfunctional mindset. I operated out of a thinking do others the way you have been done. I was operating from the knowledge of unforgiveness and being broke. That mindset came from not having enough and always doing without. I resolved to the notion I would allow someone else to figure out the financial piece. I never thought much about the respect part because from my perspective it was never an aspect of my upbringing. My father didn't respect my mother. Why should I show respect to anyone? He actually had none for us or he would have chosen to fight for his marriage and make it right. All I wanted was what I had missed out on -- love, affection, nice things, money, a beautiful home with a nice car and I wanted to travel around the world modeling. I saw how all this worked simply by watching from afar. I figured it didn't matter if the man was married or not, he could still take care of my needs and others as well. Of course, I didn't find any of this to be true. Ladies or gentlemen, if you are in a relationship with someone else's mate ask yourself, *Why*? Now follow that answer with what is controlling you to cause you to do such a drastic measure of humiliating and disrespecting yourself. You may not want to admit it, but it's time to do some soul searching. Marriage wasn't on my radar at the time. It was my belief that single women allowed other people's husbands or boyfriends to care for them and their children for years and it appeared to have made their lives so much easier. As I said, "my belief". It is not true. If your thought process is as warped as mine was- then you are on the road to deceit, manipulation, hurt, and most of all, sadness from God. The reason I say sadness from God is because scripture identifies God as Love. Hurting other people isn't love. *He that loveth not knoweth not God; for God is love* (1 John 4:48)

I began to ask myself why hadn't Mom figured this out so we could benefit and not struggle. When the struggle is affecting your life, you just want it fixed. The show, *Iyanla: Fix My Life,* we could have been the perfect family chosen for that one. Maybe Mom had started to figure it out. Maybe that's why she wasn't bothered by the many girlfriends Dad had. Maybe when she left on the weekend, she was handling her own business. Who knows what went on behind closed doors. I never questioned my mom's whereabouts or her plans. All we knew was Mom did what she had to do to care for her seven children with or without the help of our father. As children, we take in what we see and create our own illusion of the story in hopes of a happy ending. I had been brainwashed about what a *kept woman* was.

Chapter 4

Q:

Can rejection cause self-doubt?

A:

Absolutely. Rejection is a form of not being accepted.

The rejection experience can cause you to gravitate to wrong strongholds when you are dealing with unworthiness.

NOW LET'S WRITE
YOUR ANSWERS

_____

_____

_____

_____

_____

_____

_____

_____

_____

_____

_____

_____

_____

_____

_____

_____

_____

_____

_____

_____

_____

_____

_____

Chapter 5

What's Next?

By the age of nine, I was taller than the average fifth grader. Standing tall, I felt awkward amongst my classmates. I was withdrawn and spoke with a faint whisper. Since I was so tall, I slouched when I walked to look shorter. Mama always told me to stand tall and walk with confidence. She knew exactly what I was experiencing since I had her height. Years later, I realized my height was a great tool and I learned to embrace it with grace. I really thought one day I was going to be a fashion runway model and own an empire. Fast forward years later, I became my own self-proclaimed fashion model and occasionally have taken the runway. As for owning my empire, I'm on God's timing with that.

I did things average little girls did at my age. I spent a lot of time baking cakes in my easy bake oven, playing with my dolls or preparing homemade French fries. We had a potato chopper that diced each potato into the perfect French fry, which I smothered in ketchup. I loved getting all the praises of how great a job I did on cooking for my siblings. There was something about being rewarded for something you love doing. Fun in the kitchen was normally done on the weekend when Mom was gone because I wasn't supposed to use hot oil in the kitchen without any assistance. Mom always left the house saying, "Don't burn down my house cooking."

I played outside as much as I could when we were allowed to. One rule was if you go outside you stay outside. I didn't care if it was freezing cold outside, we were getting out of the house. When it was hot, Mama made us stay in the house until the sun went down. I guess she didn't like the doors being opened and closed all the time. She said it took longer to cool the house down. As a kid, I thought that was a crazy concept. Now that I'm older and wiser, I do understand what she meant. We had to come home as soon as the streetlight came on and play in the backyard when Mom wasn't home. That was a rule set for most of us in the neighborhood. Sometimes, she would be home and we still had to play around back. All of our friends would be out front and my sister and I would run in between the houses motioning for our friends to join us around back. Most of the time they would join us unless something else was taking place out front that was more interesting. That happened quite a bit, and again my sister and I felt left behind.

My younger sister and I learned early on that sometimes we would be left to entertain each other and we were responsible for each other. No matter what we did, we managed to do it together. This thinking followed us years later into adulthood. We also tried to make sure the other one was included on most things. Now that we are much older, we each have developed our own likes and dislikes and our own group of friends. I remember my junior prom. I had to take my sister to the after party or I couldn't go. My date wasn't too thrilled about it, but I tried to act like it didn't matter. We found ourselves always encouraging each other to go whether we wanted to or not, simply because our outings were limited. If we both went, it was much easier for Mom to say yes. Carlotta had a temper and a mean streak that sometimes appeared out of the blue sky. I'm sure she would beg to differ. I honestly believe she was always trying to prove herself to everyone to get noticed. Carlotta was the youngest in the house and probably never truly had a say in anything unless she was winning a fight. She made her mark as being the little Ali, the famous fighter. She was also a tomboy and didn't care much about all the frills. I was into enough of that for both of us. Although my relationships with all of my sisters were quite different, we all demonstrated the same level of love for one another but she was and still is my shadow. You hurt, I hurt. You cry, I cry. You take revenge, I help. You succeed, I succeed. We all needed the love of our absentee father and each of us sought it out the best way we knew how. Since this is my story, I will not go into details of how others reached for acceptance.

By age thirteen, I had been bullied and chased home every other day. Girls were jealous of me for reasons I never understood. They were so mean and annoying. I remember being intentionally bumped in the hall and being loudly talked about. I was not a popular girl in school or even a smart one, so the odds were already against me on top of being raised by a single mom. I was an average student that sat quietly in class hoping never to be called on by the teacher even when I knew the correct answer. Something about being singled out made me feel uncomfortable. The thought of making a mistake in front of the entire classroom made me feel like a big loser, so I remained silent. My confidence level was extremely low. I remained tall for my age and I always felt like people were making fun of my height. I wore a size nine and a half shoe and I was knock kneed and wore large frame glasses. At the time I got them, I actually thought they were cute until I overheard someone talking about my eyewear. We can be fine with ourselves until someone else decides to voice their opinions and thoughts. Since my confidence level was low that was all I needed to reassure my self-doubt. Be careful about what you say about others, words can be hurtful. Ask yourself, are my comments about others helpful or hurtful? That's something to consider before you join in on any conversation.

I had fair skin and wavy hair. They called it good hair compared to most. Actually, I inherited my complexion and hair from my dad. I resembled my dad a lot when I was younger. Now as an adult, I look more and more like my mom. I gravitated to the quiet students like myself, and the ones that were treated differently. I have always had a heart for all people, trying to make someone feel better even when I was hurting on the inside. Mom said that behavior definitely came from dad, always helping everyone out before helping himself. Mom always reminded me that I looked like my dad and possessed a free spirit like him as well. I didn't know if that was a good or a bad thing. I considered myself to be thoughtful and considerate of all and my free spirit was a part of me. I'm pretty sure Mom didn't think Dad was thoughtful or considerate to us.

A young man in one of my classes was picked on every day because he had an unpleasant body odor. I believe he was a bed wetter. I befriended him and found myself standing up for him when the other boys and girls picked on him. I always told him to ignore the insults and they would eventually stop. One day after school before we got on the bus, he had had enough. One of our classmates hit him upside the head with a snowball. Of course, everyone laughed at him except me. He began to cry and then he started fighting with everything he had inside of him. They never picked on him anymore after that. I guess I became his friend because I thought we had a lot in common, the underdogs against the world. I really felt that way as a child and an adult on various occasions. It depended on who I was around or what was being said. I knew what it felt like to be talked about and left behind. I wonder what ever happened to my dear ole friend. There will come a time in your life you will be forced to fight. As Yolanda Adams sings, "The Battle is Not Yours, It's the Lord's". What battles are you fighting? The battles I was fighting felt like they would never end, one after another. I finally realized was I was fighting a battle against myself, a battle that had me doomed for defeat and had labeled me as an outcast. Once you can identify your battles, you can begin to deal with them. My classmate identified whom he was battling and made a conscious effort that he no longer wanted to be fearful. His battle was fear.

My class schedule was pretty easy except for gym, which I disliked. I wasn't athletic so I was always chosen last to be on any team. Already feeling rejected, being chosen last all the time merely added to my pain. I realized later on in life that there are always people seeking to take advantage of others' insecurities. So, all of my insecurities started to manifest slowly. Then as I matured, I encountered even more rejection. It seemed like the initial rejection from my dad was a reminder that maybe I wasn't good enough for anyone. That rejection level was a beast. What I realize is, rejection is inevitable. Everyone isn't going to like or accept you. And rejection isn't an indicator of who you are. The problem with rejection for me was I saw rejection as something I did wrong. It really wasn't about me… or you.

I remember my mother jokingly describing how I almost killed her during childbirth because I was a breech baby. I didn't think it was funny. Actually, being told I acted like the man who had walked off and left everyone and that I almost killed my mom use to hurt my feelings. I felt completely rejected, in addition to my other issues of having an absentee father. Mom wasn't trying to be mean, she lacked tact when it came to expressing herself. But, I was only thirteen. What did I know about child birthing a breech child?

Although Mom was candid about everything and strict, one thing she tried to instill in each of us was to always be informed about what was happening in the world, to be knowledgeable about what takes place in other countries so we wouldn't be in the dark about things. She always told us knowledge was power. She encouraged us to read and be able to count money so people couldn't cheat us. We always had to count money back to her. She would sometimes ask how much money was lying on her dresser. I used to think it was a trick question to see if we would steal from her. And on occasion, I did take a few extra coins from the bottom of her handbag when she told me to get her purse, which I used to buy candy. Although I knew it was wrong. I wondered how she became so smart considering she dropped out of school early. She blasted the news or anything dealing with politics on the TV. Sometimes, she made us come in her room, sit quietly on the floor and watch the unfolding details of what was happening in our city, our country and our neighborhood. Of course, none of us listened at the time. We were too young to care about world news or any news for that matter. All we wanted to do was be kids and play outside.

After a few summers went by, our father's next door visits became scarce. The lady next door was no longer his girlfriend, but trust me, he had a new one. This one was not as pretty, but she could cook. At least that's what Dad said. I didn't like her that well because it appeared she tried too hard to be around us. Every time he dropped by the house, she was always in the front seat. We could never talk with him in private without her being present. One Saturday, he asked if we could attend a family reunion in Paola, Kansas. This particular time we were allowed to go not knowing the girlfriend would be in the car. That was the longest ride ever. She was always saying *Charles, do you think the girls want this or that.* We were angry at her for intruding on our time with our father. I ignored her when she talked to me and interrupted when she had my dad's attention. I figured the least she could do was sit quietly. I guess we were not the only ones wanting his attention. One summer, we asked for brand new bikes and got them. We were so excited Dad was taking us to get new bikes for the summer. But guess who came along for the ride? She ruined the whole trip. We later found out she was instrumental in us getting those lovely bikes. So there was a blessing behind her being involved with my dad. We got new bikes for the summer. As a child my behavior of mistreating dad's girlfriend was a demonstration of being jealous of her relationship with him. My thoughts about her didn't allow me to even get to know her, although she was willing. What behaviors do you need to let go off so you can experience being kept? I was holding on to jealous and envy.

Our once large household of eight dwindled down to four. Joe was sent away to live in Detroit with his dad because he was in and out of jail. He had started bringing his slick, good for nothing friends around the house. Mom knew she had to get him out of Kansas City before it was too late. Rene also moved out. Mama said grown women could not live together. Remember Mom was fourteen when she had Rene, therefore they kind of acted more like sisters instead of mother and daughter until Mom had to stand her ground and give Rene a beat down, that I heard was well deserved. Marsha had graduated from high school, married and moved away with her new husband. We were sad that our family was shrinking. Marsha was the glue that held us together. She was the go to person for everything. She kept Mama off our backs. Delano also got married and joined the army. He went far away to the DC area, we missed him. He was the peacemaker and the positive male presence our home needed. Tina remained home until she was sixteen. Then she decided to put on somebody else's shoes that led her to Las Vegas, Nevada. She never returned home again except to visit. Carlotta and I finally had our own bedrooms. We were able to fix them up anyway we wanted. We also had our own private telephone line. Mom was tired of our friends calling the house and decided to have an additional line put in. She finally had a full-time job that paid her a decent salary. With that, we were able to have a little more of something that the others didn't get, things like a Florida vacation and an occasional dinner at Crown Center. Our style of clothing started to change. Mom's financial status had changed. What was still missing was the sense of belonging and fitting in with others and the relationship with my Dad.

Chapter 5

Q:

What's Next for you?
What are you plans now that the truth has been
revealed?

A:

I need you to take that step and move forward.

NOW LET'S WRITE
YOUR ANSWERS

_____
_____
_____
_____
_____
_____
_____
_____
_____
_____
_____
_____
_____
_____
_____
_____
_____
_____
_____
_____
_____
_____
_____
_____
_____

Chapter 6

Is This Really Love?

I developed into a beautiful young lady. Though still tall and clumsy, by the time I turned sixteen, the boys in the neighborhood that once teased me started taking more notice in me. I wasn't sure if the attention was genuine or if they had finally grown up and decided to stop teasing me. As I got older, I realized the ones who teased me actually had a crush on me. I lived in a close-knit neighborhood therefore everyone knew what was going on in everyone's household -- the good, the bad, the truth and the lies. Some things I still wish no one knew, but the past is just that...the past. Since I had developed close friendships with most of the boys on our block, I never even gave them a second thought about being my boyfriend. I treated them all like they were my brothers. Besides, they never let on that they even liked me. Once I realized I was capable of drawing the

71

eye of the boys, I figured I had finally arrived. I made a conscious decision to step up my game and see what happened. Although my wardrobe was limited, I managed to look quite cute on those hot summer days. I wore the perfect pair of denim shorts with a purple halter top. My sister and I had a matching set. Her top was red. We always had matching everything.

One particular summer day I was all dolled up and looking quite cute. If my dad had seen me, he would have said, "My daughter is so pretty." This was something he generally said to all of his girls. So, being pretty worked for and against me. In this case, it worked for me. I caught the eye of a young gentleman that lived three blocks over. He began to visit me every evening. He was a couple of years older and went to a different school. That was perfect, because I didn't want him to know I was being teased, chased home from school and bullied by many. After weeks of conversation, we decided to make it official. I had landed my first boyfriend. I was excited. Even better, he had two parents in the same household. I thought that was such an amazing thing to be raised by both parents. He introduced me to his mom, dad and all of his brothers and sisters. We had nothing in common except for our innocence, but we were sure that we were perfect for each other. I finally introduced him to my mom. She made no comment about it other than, "I know you don't call yourself having a boyfriend. I told you once already you are not old enough." *Old enough*, I thought. How old did I have to be to have a boyfriend? I was a junior in high school. My response was always, "No, ma'am. We're just friends." Of course, she knew differently. She had been my age before and knew exactly what I was dealing with. I think my mom tried to act like she was in the dark, but she wasn't.

Even though Mom didn't ask a lot of questions, she was watchful of all her girls. I think she paid a little more attention than she let on. I remember she would ask my older sisters about their monthly menstrual cycle, "Did y'all get your period this month?" I thought it was an odd question but later realized the question made you think about what you were doing or what you shouldn't be doing. She explained the birds and the bees to me in her direct and very blunt way. She made it clear if you missed your menstrual cycle it meant you were doing something you should not have been doing and you were in big trouble. Mom felt it was not needed by her to go into depth about sex considering I had older siblings that could inform me. What she didn't know was they were doing their own life and I was sneaky and secretive. How could I possibly have a conversation about something that no one ever talked about? I could get the answer about a relationship between a man and a woman by watching others from afar. The necessary details weren't important or so I thought.

I learned a lot by paying close attention to my older siblings and my surroundings. By watching my oldest sister Rene, I knew to never get caught skipping school. Marsha taught me how to pray. Every night she held me accountable to prayer. Tina introduced me to makeup. I secretly watched how red or black lipstick changed your entire look. My brother Delano taught me everything wasn't that serious and laughter could cover up a lot. I had many examples to help me along the way, some good and some bad. The biggest defeat was me. I was insecure, shy, looking to belong somewhere and be accepted by all. The many examples of life that was before me, I used a little here and a little there. Everything I retained was not implemented properly. Being sneaky and making myself look older gained me the attention I thought I needed. I started attending evening church services with my boyfriend and enjoyed hanging out with him doing nothing. I stopped waiting for my dad to drive down our block, replacing the wait with something and somebody else. I believe Mom liked my boyfriend and allowed me to spend so much time with him because we were mainly at church with his family. She probably thought she didn't have to worry about what I was doing because I was supposed to be at church. What she didn't know was sometimes we didn't always attend the evening services. We did our own thing. Most of our time together was spent talking, laughing, hanging out in the park or watching TV. Every chance I got I made an excuse to walk around the corner and see him. He would sneak on my block to see me as well. Despite all of our sneaking around, pretty soon everyone knew we were a couple. When the street lights came on it was time for me to come in the house, but I always managed to sneak back out. We spent hours talking and laughing right outside the front of the house until the wee hours of the morning.

Mom had a way of keeping track of us by setting the home burglar system. In order to get out of the house, we had to shut the system down from inside her bedroom. We learned quickly how to come up with an excuse on why we needed to disarm the system. Mom never questioned us, so we were able to sneak outside without being caught. Of course, we never went far just on the front porch. I say we because Carlotta and I worked as a team. We always had to come in the house earlier than everyone else, usually about the time the fun was just getting started.

Since there were no strong male role models in my life, the experiences with boys was trial and error. My newfound love gave me the needed attention I never received from my father. He taught me how to drive in his brand new silver Regal with the nice T-top sunroof. We went out to dinner and I watched him perform with his band. Everything I could imagine was coming true. He bought me things and showed up every day on the bus stop to meet me after school. We made a decision that we would commit ourselves to each other and one day we gave in to the desires of our flesh. Our relationship grew and flourished. We became attached to each other every day. Suddenly, our world changed and the confusion started. My menstrual cycle was late and I was scared to death. I was only sixteen and he was eighteen. What had I done? My worst nightmare had come to light. What I had done in the dark was about to be revealed. What were we going to tell our parents? Surely, I wasn't pregnant. My mom had already told me if my cycle was ever late I was in big trouble. Since he was a senior in high school getting ready to graduate, he decided to tell his parents there was a possibility his girlfriend was pregnant. They told him he needed to do the right thing by both of us, join the Navy and marry me after I graduated. It turned out I was not pregnant, but his mind was already committed to the Navy so he left me. I was devastated. The one who said he loved me would soon be gone. I felt betrayed again. The feelings of loss, rejection, fear, and abandonment resurfaced. We continued our relationship from afar, but it eventually ended after he finished boot camp. He was slipping out with other people and I had gotten wind of it through a slip of the tongue by his mom. I never felt I was the one his mom would have picked for him. She wanted more for her son and I wasn't it. I believed my background of being raised by a single mom had a lot to do with how she felt. Our childhood relationship ended and I placed him in the danger zone along with all the other cheating, lying men I had watched. After that, I decided MEN could not be trusted. Years later, the truth was revealed about what really happened. We both were too young for the commitment we had promised each other. Being kept from the truth hurts.

Senior year in high school I was taller, much cuter, very skinny but shapely. I was no longer being chased home or made fun of. I managed to keep my hair looking stylish and my clothes were more fashionable. I was still shy and insecure but attempting to grow into my own beautiful self, trying to fit in wherever I could. I was still missing my absentee father but trying to cope. The attention from my dad surfaced by way of a promised gift.

Dad had promised all of the girls a brand-new diamond watch for graduation so I was on target to receive my BLING. That was the first special gift I ever received from my father at the age of seventeen. I was able to graduate midterm therefore I only had half days and was allowed to leave school early. Afraid my mom would make me come home and work around the house, I didn't tell her. Since there were only two of us at home, I refused to go home and take care of all the chores by myself. With the principal's approval, I was able to be an office assistant half of the day. I spent a lot of time in the office running errands and working around the entire staff.

Being an insecure young girl, I was flattered by any and all compliments paid to me, especially if they came from a male. I remember thinking *I must really be special getting all of this attention*. They always told me how pretty I was and that I carried myself like a young lady. Most of them were sincere and professional, although there was one particular incident. As I was leaving one afternoon, the security guard handed me his number and told me not to tell anyone. He offered to take me to dinner one evening if I was available. I thought that was strange of him considering he was old and married. What was he up too? I had already noticed he always talked to the young girls outside while he was taking a smoking break. I guess he made moves on all the young girls, including me. I never called him and he became a little irritated with me and started making me feel uncomfortable anytime I walked by him. Anytime I saw him in the hallway, I changed my direction even if it meant making me late to class. One day he finally cornered me on the staircase and asked why I took his number if I wasn't going to use it. His tone was strong and authoritative. The only authority I was taught to adhere by was my mom. I didn't report this incident to anyone out of fear of getting in trouble with my mom for taking his telephone number. She had warned me time after time to stay away from boys, always calling me a fast tail. It made me think I may have encouraged him in some way, which I didn't, I was actually innocent. Even if I dressed older and wore makeup, he knew my age and that I was a student in high school. I heard later he was fired for sexual harassment filed by a teacher on behalf of another student. I wish I had spoken up for myself at that time. I thank God for keeping me.

Several different men tried to approach me, but I knew it wasn't right. What was wrong with me? Did I have a sign on my back saying very insecure, in need of a father figure, lost and confused? You name it. I was receiving attention everywhere. Men were coming full steam ahead and I was only seventeen years old. I think what kept me out of trouble was all these men were all old and I was afraid of getting caught and having to explain to my mother what I had done. The fear of my mom was strong! I wonder if my father had played an active role in my life, would I have sought attention from these boys or old geezers.

I graduated from high school and received my diamond watch as promised by my dad. He finally came through on what he said. Maybe things were starting to look up for me. It was nice being given a gift that represented LOVE. Do gifts really represent love or was it the fact my dad gave it to me? As I look at my diamond Bulova watch, it is a constant reminder that your word is key. Thank you Lord for allowing my dad to keep his word and promise. What promises have you made to yourself or to others? Did you keep your promise? It is never too late to make good on a promise.

Chapter 6

Q:

Do you love yourself ?
Write down ways you demonstrate love for yourself.

A:

Now, I do!

NOW LET'S WRITE
YOUR ANSWERS

_____

_____

_____

_____

_____

_____

_____

_____

_____

_____

_____

_____

_____

_____

_____

_____

_____

_____

_____

_____

_____

_____

_____

Chapter 7

Being Preyed Upon

I was all grown up and no one could tell me anything. I had my high school diploma so I was done with school for now. I was getting attention from much older men and boys my age, while still trying to find my way in this new adult season. Something about the way I walked was different. My walk demonstrated confidence but truthfully, I had none. Every time I walked around the corner to the neighborhood candy store, I passed this one particular house. A gentleman always sat on the porch. He would wave and smile at me when I walked by. On occasion, he made small talk asking me where I lived. Since I traveled this path on a regular basis, I became more comfortable talking with him. I thought he looked okay. He always addressed me as *Ms. Lady* and I liked that. I thought the way he addressed me meant I was representing the ladies I had envisioned in the past. The ladies that had style and class and were beautiful.

He had several beautiful cars parked in the driveway. I assumed they were his since he made it clear he was single and lived alone. Somewhere in the conversation, he shared with me he owned his home. Although the home was quite small, it was neat with a well-groomed yard. Every day I started to engage in more and more conversation with him trying to act like I wasn't interested in him. I should have backed up once he told me he had two daughters, but I didn't. I was still eager to get to know him much better. One day he asked me if I wanted to go skating with him and some friends. I told him I had to ask my mom. He retorted, "Aren't you out of high school?" As though me asking my mother was adolescent. I knew I couldn't ask my mom about going skating with a total stranger, so I lied and told her I was going with someone else and snuck out with him anyway. The ability to lie to get my way was a learned behavior I had picked up from many. I found myself hanging out around the corner more frequently and over time, I became fascinated with his slick conversation and his means to buy me a few trinkets here and there. Actually, that's all it was. I never allowed it to be anything more significant. When men told me I was pretty, I thought they were sincere. Some also said we could make pretty babies together. At first, I was flattered. I thought it was a cute compliment. I was naïve and didn't even realize it was a disrespectful comment for a man to say to a woman that wasn't his wife. I started learning how to use my charm to get what I wanted. I got rides to work, perfume and birthday cards. I was getting all kinds of stuff, things I had witnessed as a child and interpreted as I was being taken care of. At eighteen-years-old, I had the attention of a twenty-six year old man. Was he seriously interested in little ole me? Was it love or was it my charming ways? Was it the intelligent conversation we shared? Maybe I was special. Or maybe it was the sex. Was he was going to marry me? I knew it wasn't any of the above. All of the signs were evident in the way he treated me, demonstrating his attraction to me when it was only beneficial for him. I had placed myself in a situation that allowed me to be used and taken advantage of. Although I was lacking self-esteem, self-worth and insecurities while in search of being loved, I still should have known better.

The writing was on the wall when he started asking me for money to put gas in his car. It never failed; whenever he picked me up from work he always warned me beforehand that he might need gas. If only I had told somebody, perhaps someone who cared might have said, "Rochinda you are deserving of the best of everything." As I reflect back, I was manipulated to believe he was doing me a favor by picking me up because I actually had no other way home at times if my Mom couldn't pick me up. He demonstrated a behavior I had seen and heard about from afar. Mom on occasion called my dad a womanizer. She would mention that dad had women around that could help achieve whatever he wanted. I didn't want to believe that about my dad, but I had seen it from my neighborhood watch parties. My mom never liked the guy I was seeing therefore I couldn't tell her the truth. He was my outlet on the weekend for having a little fun. She said he was too old and was street slick. Me being young and seeking attention, I didn't listen to her. I got caught up with all the fascinating parties, the money, and the cool cars. I thought it was cute being able to hang out with the older crowd. I remembered my dad being older than my mother and it wasn't a big deal. I found out this man had a girlfriend and had being lying to both of us.

As you may notice, I repeat over and over how I was lost, confuse, insecure and yearning for attention.

I was trying to fit in wherever I could. I didn't know my self-worth. I thought because he gave me shiny little trinkets and gifts that was love. I had nothing of great significance to compare it to. I once received a beautiful watch from my dad that was a reflection of love. I watched how my dad interacted with all his lady friends who appeared to be in love with him. How did I allow myself to be captured by this man's skillful premeditated prey? An imposter who knew exactly what to look for in his victims had preyed upon me. Why hadn't my mother or father prepared me for this? The brief conversations I had with my mom never ended in the disclosure of how to identify an imposter. My mom revealed to me that all men were imposters of some sort. I believe her relationship with my dad had much to do with her thoughts. Why hadn't my brothers clued me in on the opposite sex? My brothers weren't equipped themselves. They both were long gone living their own lives. I was left to walk straight into the lion's den to be eaten up and spit back out. I had free will not to even enter into the den, but I blindly walked in anyway. I was in search of something much greater. I just didn't know exactly where to look or where to go. I needed my father.

The summer of 1982 I enjoyed a little bit too much. I should have been preparing to go off to college, but I wasn't. Instead, I was being prepared for motherhood. On December 27, 1983, I gave birth to a beautiful baby girl weighing seven pounds and two and three quarters ounces. She was eighteen and a half inches long. I was nineteen years old and completely clueless. I knew nothing about becoming a mother. All I knew was what I had seen by my mother and the neighborhood moms. I knew nothing about breastfeeding or even taking a baby's temperature. Whatever I didn't know, I was determined to learn.

I remember the day I found out I was pregnant and the moment I had to tell my mom. My mother only asked me one question, "Rochinda, what do you want to do?" I responded, "What do you mean what do I want to do?" She asked, "Do you want to have this baby?" I started crying and said, "ABSOLUTELY! This is my baby. I plan to raise her and give her the best life ever, even if it means doing that by myself." My mom wanted me to know she was supportive of whatever decision I made, right or wrong. Trust me, I made the right choice.

I told the father I was pregnant, but he went into denial mold saying it wasn't his baby and asking me what was I going to do, like I had gotten pregnant on my own. I was crushed because I knew who the father was. There was no shadow of doubt. After I got over the initial shock of being rejected once again, my heart became numb and resentment and anger set in. I decided my baby's daddy didn't exist and made up in my mind my daughter was my gift from God, my own little baby doll. After she was born, he did stop by with some formula and diapers. I graciously accepted, but I knew I had to disconnect my daughter and myself from any more rejection, hurt and abandonment. Years later, I was told by my daughter that her biological father claims he didn't realize a baby had been born as that was a dark time in his life. I guess the recollection of ever stopping by to see her didn't count. I learned from my mom not to talk bad about my daughter's biological father and to allow her to develop her own relationship when she decided to. Again, being kept by drugs, women, lies, and hurt will keep you in bondage. These are many examples of being kept by the enemy.

After being raised by a single mom and watching her struggle with seven children, I was determined to do things differently. I decided I wasn't going to force anyone to take care of their child against their own will. Although aid was available, I didn't qualify since I was working and my income was just enough to care for the two of us. Like I said…just enough. I did qualify for assistance with daycare early on until my income structure changed by a few dollars.

I guess after my father watched me embrace being a single mom, our relationship started to develop. My dad never knew the impact of him not being there had on my life. I believe my dad saw the same strength in me that my mom had and, from time to time, I saw him watching me from afar with a smile. At that time, I knew my father loved me. I just didn't know how to fix myself of all the pain caused by others that I was harboring. I knew there had to be a solution to all of this madness, I just needed to figure it out before my baby girl aged. I remember Daddy asking me if I wanted him to apply pressure to make this guy help out with his child. He said, "Honey, I can make this guy take care of his child." All I could think was, *Really? You didn't do such a great job taking care of us. How can you do that?* But I actually answered, "No, I will handle it in due time." I didn't believe what my dad had in mind would be beneficial to anyone and could probably land him in jail.

The majority of my friends went off to college leaving me behind. They knew my struggles but couldn't do much about it. Rusha, my best friend called me as much as she could in between her classes and sent the best gifts a college student could afford for my baby girl. She never missed a birthday or a holiday. She never voiced her opinion about how she felt, but I knew I had disappointed her. We had planned to go off to college together and enjoy the college experience. My friends were pursuing their dreams of higher education and I should have been a part of that adventure.

Feeling rejected, left behind, lost, and confused, I turned my attention toward home. My daughter and I had needs that needed to be met. My baby was growing rapidly and outgrowing everything. I had maxed out my Macy's credit card and emptied out the little bit of savings I had. Being so young, I didn't realize the importance of paying your bills on time. I learned the hard way, but eventually figured it out. When it came to my baby girl, the sky was the limit. I had experienced a lifetime of lack and had determined this would not be her experience. When people saw us, no one knew the struggle. I learned firsthand by my mother, everybody didn't have to know your struggles. Again, I was in denial of the truth of what was needed in my life.

My baby girl wasn't old enough to miss a father image so I had time to fix it. As I set out to find or make a life for my daughter and I, older gentlemen that reminded me of my father always approached me. They had the same ole line and the same old story. Once you heard it, you recognized it. What is that saying, *game recognizes game*. Their pick-up line sounded like this, "Hey, pretty lady. Young tenderoni." Really? *Tenderoni*. What was that all about? It sounded like they were hungry or something. I was nineteen with a baby and broke and all they could say was, "You're pretty." The same ole, same ole.

My mom always told me to stay away from men who only focused on my beauty. She constantly reminded me beauty would eventually fade and not to pay attention to the hype of how beautiful you are. I remember as I got older mom fussing at my dad about telling his girls they were pretty. She would say, "Charles, you need to fill their head with something more than all of that nonsense." Even though she told me that, I still craved to hear those words. I had a deep yearning to be complimented by a male. Some men even went as far as wanting to help me become financially stable. When I heard that, I knew it was more to it. It was no longer just about me. I had a beautiful baby girl I had to take care of. I couldn't allow just anybody in her presence. I had to make sure her mind ouldn't be contaminated like mine. Although

I was young, I was now responsible for shaping and molding another life. I knew the choices I made in my relationships could help or hurt us so I had to be particularly selective. My thoughts were on point and precise. Turns out, these men were married or in a relationship. Since I had witnessed enough of that, I knew that was not the answer for me. I didn't have time to waste. I had watched and studied the behavior of married men for years. I saw firsthand how they treated their wives, mistresses and children. I find those who believe it's ok and blame their wives for the unacceptable behavior so appalling. Some of us have allowed ourselves to be kept by someone else's mate in order to feel good about ourselves. I'm sure this happens to men as well, but I'm speaking to the ladies on this particular issue.

I was in a rage. Rejected. Betrayed. Lost. Confused. I was angry, fearful of being cheated on by my boyfriend and frustrated with two absentee fathers. I had no one to talk to. Everyone else had gone on with their lives. It was time for me to take some action. I wanted revenge. I wanted to get even, but I wanted to do it the legal way. How could I locate all the deadbeat dads in the universe? This was going to take some time. How long did I have? Where would I start? I needed a full-time job that paid me well. As quickly as the above questions were thrown out at me, my response was even quicker. I responded with urgency that some would say was extreme. I wanted revenge on the men in the universe, that's a massive quest. Besides that, all of these men had not done me wrong, but I didn't care. I felt like the few was enough. I had no idea what I was up against or if I could even pull this off. In order to locate anyone, I would need public records with all of their information. While orchestrating all of this, I needed to get paid as well to provide for my daughter and me.

I applied for a job at the police department, not just any job, but a position as a police officer. That was it. I would be intentional in tracking down all the losers in the world making babies and leaving them behind. I was determined to help put a stop to all of the madness that was created in the lives of vulnerable women and children. Didn't these deadbeat dads understand the damage they had caused in the lives of vulnerable women and children? The definition of deadbeat is a person who tries to evade paying debts; a loafer, one who persistently fails to pay personal debts or expenses. There are some deadbeat women too, but my search was for the men. Didn't they know their daughters were supposed to look up to them? I looked up to my dad, although he wasn't around much and I feel like I was disappointed by his actions. Didn't they know fathers were supposed to provide for their families? Being able to provide for your own family meant commitment to do the hard work, not bail out and leave, like I had been. Didn't they know girls watch how their fathers treat their moms? Didn't they know girls were supposed to receive their first flowers and first dance from their dad? The flowers and dance meant you were special. That representation is carried over into life. Didn't they know little girls grow up to be grown women who needed a great reference point? The first role model a little girl has is supposed to be represented in a positive manner. If any of these men actually knew the extent of the impact they made in the life of a young girl, do you think they would have done something differently? I don't have all of the answers but what I know for sure is I had been in bondage for most of my life at that point. I needed a solution that could help all the broken-hearted women and abandoned children.

Chapter 7

Q:

People who prey upon others. Are they broken?

A:

Absolutely. Hurt people hurt others.

NOW LET'S WRITE
YOUR ANSWERS

_____
_____
_____
_____
_____
_____
_____
_____
_____
_____
_____
_____
_____
_____
_____
_____
_____
_____
_____
_____
_____
_____
_____
_____

Chapter 8

Seek and You Shall Have

The police department hired me. My family threw me a big party. All my friends, new and old, came to the big celebration. There was cake, balloons, ice cream, fake handcuffs and a toy water gun. Finally, my plan was coming together. No one knew my intentions. No one knew of the hidden agenda tucked deeply inside of me. Not one person discovered my deep dark secret. They didn't know what was brewing behind the false smiling face. I had presented the most intriguing heartwarming honorable story ever. I was going to make a difference in the world.

Since I had grown up in a household with a single mom, I expressed to all that single parents needed to have protection while they were home alone tending to their families. I went as far as saying that since my oldest brother had been in and out of the system, I needed to give time back to the community as much as I could. Most everyone thought I was trying to save the world, but my sister Marsha knew something else was beneath this farce. She couldn't pinpoint it, but she knew her baby sister was lost and confused and she was well aware that I wasn't cut out for police work. I never shared with her the inner truth because I was afraid she would try to talk me out of it or at least tell Mom. I couldn't divulge to anyone that I was trying to locate the deadbeat dads that had left us in this world. I knew there were many other women like myself that needed an advocate on their behalf.

Mom told my father I had been hired by the police department. It wasn't much he could say since he was a big part of the damaged roots that had taken life from my spirit, heart and core. My father didn't realize his broken commitment to my mother haunted me every single day. The way he took notice of others over me was almost unbearable. The way he ran all over town with different women and later, when I found out a few of my classmates were his drinking buddies, was heartbreaking. How dare he give me advice on what was good for my daughter and me? His actions displayed throughout my life taught me to never trust men. He showed me how to get what I wanted by using my charm and beauty. I heard him repeatedly say how pretty I was. Therefore, when anyone told me that, I believed it. As far as I was concerned, he taught me exactly how to treat men. My thinking was way off. I was an angry, mad, insecure single mom who needed someone to blame. While in the police academy, I started developing more strength day by day to achieve my set goal.

I stood tall with confidence, weighing 125 pounds as I reported to the academy. I learned how to defend myself, fire a handgun and shoot with accuracy. I learned how to keep up with the best and bring down an overweight male. I learned my challenges could be defeated. Every day I encountered something new and more challenging. Driving the police car at high speed and going on a ride along was captivating. One thing about the police academy, your charm or beauty won't get you too far, not even the batting of your eyes. You could not wiggle your way through. Deep down inside of my soul, like my sister, I knew I wasn't cut out for police work. But the revenge was so embedded in me, I continued to move forward.

Then the day came when I hit a roadblock. I had a problem with one of the teachers in the academy. She constantly reminded me that I would not finish because I wasn't cut out for this kind of work. She was the instructor from hell, racist and mean. I tried to stay away from her because she had actually read me right. I really wasn't cut out for the academy. All I wanted was access to what I thought freedom was, revenge against deadbeat dads. Although I had a plan, God had one too. I failed out of the academy one week prior to graduation. Can you believe that? I had to meet with the police board. As I walked into the boardroom, my stomach had a knot in it. I knew this wasn't going to be a good meeting. I had witnessed this with other fellow cadets who received their walking papers. In the boardroom, I was told, "Sorry, Rochinda, you have not met the requirements to become a police officer." I was like: *Are you kidding me? Do you realize I have a mission that must be fulfilled? I have an assignment to reap havoc on all the deadbeat dads that have reaped havoc on all the women in their lives and their children by abandoning them. If I can't be on the streets, how will I accomplish this mission? What would I do now?* The what was a serious question. I did not prepare for failure. This job would be my saving grace in many areas of my life, provision for my daughter and access to data I needed to help complete my mission.

One of the board members spoke sternly, "You can go back through the academy when another class starts. In the meantime, apply for a jailer position." I looked at her, another sister who held the rank of Major. I was thinking, *You are supposed to be on my side. Can't you give a sister another chance? What is it going to hurt? I know the material. I'm just not a good test taker. I don't have much time to study. I have a beautiful daughter I must take care of. Besides, I'm in search of all the men who broke their promises. We sisters need to stick together.* All of this played out in my head, but what came out of my mouth was, "Thank you for this opportunity to participate in the police academy program. If I choose to pursue a career with the police department, I will reapply." As I walked out of the door, I was sick to my stomach. I let out a loud silent scream. I couldn't believe I had wasted months in training and study for it to end like this.

I felt like I was on the road to hell. I was going to have to find a job immediately. My daughter and I lived with my sister Marsha and her babies at the time. Marsha's marriage had ended in divorce causing her a setback in life. We needed each other financially and for moral support. Mom was renting the house to us that we once lived in as children and had purchased a brand-new home, where she and my baby sister now lived. After the birth of my baby, I was home with Mom for about six months, but we needed our own space so I moved in with my sister.

While in the police academy, I had made friends with some of the other cadets. One in particular help me along the way. I guess the tutoring wasn't helpful since I couldn't pass all of the required testing. I was in a dark place after being dismissed from the academy. I was an unemployed, single mom looking for love, security and a father figure for my daughter and I. I needed someone who was nice and respectable that would love and care for me.

I met with my friend from the academy occasionally for breakfast at Denny's. I paid for my meal and he paid for his. I was determined to act as though I had it together, although he knew I was jobless. We never talked about us as a couple. We considered ourselves to be good friends. We had generic conversation about the police department and what I wasn't missing. I never told him why I wanted to be a police officer. He made it clear in the academy that he would never be in a relationship with a fellow officer and to marry a cop was totally a big no no. He thought a woman's job was to be home with her family not patrolling the streets. The beliefs instilled in him came from being raised by a controlling father.

Little did he know, I was an angry, broken woman in disguise. The more we hung out and the more he talked, I started to see his positive qualities of being a provider, father, boyfriend, and possibly even a mate for marriage. But the verdict was still out. Finally, we hung out so much we established a great friendship. I only wanted to date men without children or attachments because selfishly, I wanted my daughter and I to be first all the time. I knew what it was like to be second and third. My fellow police cadet and I developed a courtship that lasted about ten months before we got married. My fairytale fantasy was finally falling in place.

My daughter and I found a sense of belonging and felt what love really was. We gained that strong male presence and firm state of financial security that had been missing from our lives. My daughter had a new grandma and grandpa, an aunt and an uncle and several other relatives that embraced us. My baby girl didn't want for anything. She had an amazing Godmother named Joann that had been with us from day one and my sisters and mother were always supportive in her upbringing. But a household with two parents present was key. I knew nothing about what a two-parent home was like other than what I saw on TV. I was raised by a single mom who did everything. Her motto was *Black woman, hear me roar. I can do anything by myself.*

I didn't want to take on that motto. I didn't want to be the woman who ran the entire house. I didn't want to lose my feminine ways. I wanted to be wined and dined. I wanted to be a stay at home mother that baked cookies and prepared meals for everyone. I wanted my home to be a place of peace and comfort. I wanted to have at least three children. I wanted a lot but never took in consideration what marriage was really about. I didn't realize being married meant you had to communicate openly with your mate about everything. I didn't realize that all of our holidays were joined with everyone's schedule. It was so much I was clueless about and I had no one to teach me.

My husband was raised by both parents. Therefore, his views and expectations were different from mine. The more I was around his family, the more fascinating his family became. They gave out big hugs and told us daily how much they loved us. I had never experienced anything like that. We went on camping trips together. I thought they looked like the All-American family. They treated my baby with royalty as she deserved. There was never a mention about who her biological father was. We finally stopped looking for her absentee father and had replaced him with a real man that she called Dad. We were finally experiencing love and being kept by a husband and father that provided our every need.

Chapter 8

Q:

What are you searching for?

A:

NOW LET'S WRITE
YOUR ANSWERS

_____
_____
_____
_____
_____
_____
_____
_____
_____
_____
_____
_____
_____
_____
_____
_____
_____
_____
_____
_____
_____
_____
_____
_____

Chapter 9

Truth

Although I was now married, I was still insecure and still holding on to rejection inside. No one would have ever known anything was wrong. I enjoyed being married. I enjoyed being taken care of and having someone else make decisions about what was needed. I had embraced this newfound life as a married woman. It was amazing how your marital status quickly changed how people viewed you. However, until you view yourself differently and change your mindset, you will always be captive to the past.

I worked outside of the home, but my husband contributed the majority of the income to our household. Together, we did fairly well for just starting out with the responsibility of our little girl. After four years of marriage, we had a son. We named him Darrell after his dad and his grandpa. That was a proud moment for the family. The family name would be carried on. I didn't understand the significance of the name thing since my father didn't seem too proud of my brother being his namesake. Honestly, I didn't know what my dad thought because that subject never came up with my brother and I. I'm sure Dad was proud of all of his sons. Even though, from my viewpoint, he just didn't show or tell them. I guess Dad didn't know how to express himself in that way.

Being a working mom took its toll on me. I came home complaining about my supervisor. The insecure little girl in me started to surface. My ability to perform at a certain level was being questioned and compared to other coworkers that had college degrees. I had graduated from high school and attended junior college for about a semester. The academy hours were equivalent to an associate degree in criminal justice. Since I was insecure and not confident with my ability to compete without a college degree any situations that dealt with education caused me to shut down and underestimate my ability. I had lots of insecurities when it came to being compared with others that appeared to be smarter than I. Those challenges I put on myself because of my own issues. After strategically putting a solid plan together to stay home and care for my family, I quit my job and became a full time stay home mom in December 1991. I was ecstatic.

My life was now shaping into one of the TV shows I had watched. It felt like one of my childhood dreams had become true. All of my friends couldn't believe I was elated to stay home. Some said eventually I would get bored and need to find an outlet. Little did they know I wanted to be home and do nothing but take care of my home. I never cared about working a nine to five, especially in an office. My childhood dreams were to be a top model and travel the world seeing fashion and meeting new people. My life as a model was eventually put to rest. I let go of that dream and picked up the new one I was now living.

It's amazing when you put your mind to something how you can succeed. I learned how to cut back on some of the things I had become accustomed to, like my hair that appointments went from weekly to every three weeks. I even cut back on my excessive shopping. After being home for two years, I had another baby girl, Andrea. I was thirty years old with a newborn, a three-year-old and an eleven-year-old; my house was full. There was hardly any time for me. My full-time position of stay at home mom started to feel more like a prisoner in my own home. Wherever I went, the children went. When we dined out, everyone's food was eaten hot except mine, which generally packaged to go. Most outings were during the day since I was home. Evenings were for homework, dinner and bath time and ended with one exhausted insecure, lost, confused stay home mom. I felt like I deserved to be home with my babies enjoying my life, so why wasn't I? I didn't have the answers nor was I trying to seek them out. I was so busy looking for someone to fix me.

My husband's career as an officer had taken off. He provided me with the stability, security, love, and compassion I had sought. Everything I thought I wanted was hand delivered to me, so what was the problem? What was missing? The attention I desired and needed was lacking but that wasn't it. The long strolls in the park weren't taking place, but that wasn't it. The children and I attended church on a regular basis. They were active in the youth programs and served as acolyte. That wasn't it. I was given a brand new fully loaded Acura MDX. That wasn't it. I was involved in all of my children's activities — track, soccer, piano, basketball, volleyball, cross country — you name it, I was there. My children attended private and one of the best Montessori schools in Kansas City. I was a room mother and sat on PTA boards. All the teachers knew my name. I was consistently at the school donating my time and trying to be accepted into this new life called *married with children*. But, something was seriously missing.

How do you ask for something when you don't know what it is that's missing? I could feel the void in my gut. I wanted to be home with my children and be the best wife I could be but slowly and surely, I started losing my identity. I started getting complacent with my appearance. I gained weight, no longer feeling attractive. I would drop the children off at school and rush home, climb in the bed and watch one of my favorite TV shows, *The Young and the Restless*. I became consumed with daytime TV. The life I had sought after began to feel empty. The husband I had married was busy working to keep the lifestyle we had created. I felt like everyone had what they needed except me. I was lost. Since I was a stay home mom, I didn't keep up on any reading like mom always told us to do unless it pertained to the kids or the courses that was being taken to help my husband obtain his degree. Everyone else appeared to have it going on. I found myself looking in the mirror at myself day in and day out. That insecure little girl appeared out of nowhere. The feeling of not belonging intruded once again. The self-doubt was strong. How was it possible to birth three children, maintain a household and keep a smile on everyone's face, yet feel empty and hopeless on the inside?

As a child, I was made fun of and talked about. My father had abandoned me when I was ten months old. My mom was too tired to hold me tight and tell me it was going to be okay. I started to feel like I was just mom, wife and housekeeper. The truth is I was a good mom and an excellent wife with great housekeeping skills. The problem wasn't anyone else's, it was my own darkness that lived inside of me. I needed validation for being, because for years I felt unnoticed. I remember going to an event that made me feel awkward. I hadn't felt like that in years. Some seemingly well-educated women that I perceived had it going on approached me. The feeling of inadequacy slipped in so quickly. I started questioning my ability to hold an intelligent conversation with people. I was afraid I would be asked that infamous question, "What do you do for a living?"

At that time in my life, I was dealing with insecurities that had lain dormant for years. I remembered attending this prestigious banquet with all of these important people and the haunting question came up again. The question I didn't know how to answer. Silence crept in. I couldn't speak. I muttered, "I'm a stay home mom." I received a look of disbelief. The smirks on people's faces were appalling. As they walked away, I remember thinking *did they just dismiss me because I said I was a stay home mom*? Actually, some of these same people are occasionally in my presence now. I don't think they meant anything by it. How would they have known of all my insecurities? My mom would use the term educated fools, but still my feelings were hurt. I was upset the rest of the evening, ready to go home and do what I did best, love on my babies because I knew they would never reject me. My babies loved me unconditionally. They didn't care if I had a degree, all they knew was I was Mama. I wondered sometimes if some of the remarks made that evening were simply because of their own envy. Of course, I wasn't convinced that was the case.

After having continuous conversations with other women, I started taking in what society thought I should do. I decided I was going to get a part time job. My husband was against me working outside of the home. He said his job was enough to support the family and we had agreed I would stay home indefinitely. What he didn't understand was I needed space and an outlet to be me. I later convinced him to allow me to sell Mary Kay. I also tried selling Black Art. Needless to say, I didn't do well because I never had a sitter to be with the children for the length of time needed. Of course that bothered me, so I had to blame someone. I was hurt that I wasn't getting the support I needed to fulfill the desire in me to achieve. I blamed the lack of support as the reason I was not accomplishing my goals. I felt like I was being controlled all over again. I had been controlled as a child, so I wasn't having it. I became a rebellious woman determined to make my point heard. I normally went along with whatever was asked of me, but I finally decided to take a stand for what I wanted. I didn't care what anyone thought. I would do my art and Mary Kay shows at home while the kids were there. Well, that was a mess. All it created was tension for the entire house.

Remember, I knew nothing about respecting a husband. I knew nothing about allowing my husband to lead or allowing a man to run anything for that matter. So there was always a tug a war going on, and I generally lost. The men that were present in my life were not good role models. My father left us. My oldest brother was in and out of jail, he had no respect for women. My younger brother moved away and never came back. Who could I call to talk to about this? Again, I was lost and confused, left to figure this out all on my own.

Our children were getting older and becoming self-sufficient and my marriage was on the rocks. The deep embedded hurt that remained in my heart caused me to overreact to everything, good and bad. It seemed we were on two different roads, a road to higher ground for him and a road to self-destruction, doubt, self-pity and selfishness for me. Our conversations turned into arguments. Arguments turned into name calling. Name calling turned into hurt. That hurt rose up again, uncovering the wound that had always been there.

The things I thought about myself had manifested out of his mouth. He had no idea I was carrying fear, rejection, pain, hurt, insecurity, mistrust and a desire for revenge around with me for years. He had no idea I had baggage that should have been revealed early on. He was clueless that I longed for my absentee father all my life. He had no idea I had been teased, taunted, and bullied in my childhood. He had no idea I struggled in school. He had no idea I craved affection and attention. He had no idea the words that came out of his mouth were a reflection of what I saw when I looked in the mirror daily.

What did he say that was so bad to cause me shut down completely? Let me explain. It wasn't just one word. It was an accumulation of buried truth. Truth that had lain dormant for years. *A man will not control me. I will not be told what to do. You are not my master or my father.* My father left me when I was ten months old. Sure, he appeared from time to time, but he still left me. The past showed up in my marriage. All of my unresolved issues manifested in our household resulting in us separating, which ended in a divorce that lasted over a year. After deep counseling and uncovering the truth on both parts of hurts and pains and the removal of the expectations we had placed on one another, we were able to start over again with a new life. We re-married and moved to a brand new house, a home I selected. I purchased brand new furniture to fill each room with what I wanted. I enrolled back into college to gain more knowledge. I started enjoying life. My oldest daughter Brittany had graduated from college and relocated to Dallas. She had gotten the footing and stability she needed to succeed in life. My son Darrell was a sophomore in high school playing football and evolving into his own identity. He was brilliant like his dad, and handsome too. Andrea was in the eighth grade enjoying volleyball, basketball, track and mastering the skills of a pianist.

In eighteen years of marriage, not including the one we lost, we had done well for ourselves. We managed to put our family back together and started worshipping together. I was employed part time for an independent electronic company that took a chance on me, giving me a sense of ownership. I had decided I would never slip back into that deep dark hole. Did you catch what I said? **I decided**. I made a conscious decision to move forward. Everything was being planned and mapped out on how things were going to happen and what our new life was going to look like. Picture perfect. My husband would make sure everything was taken care of just like before.

Chapter 9

Q:

Are you ready to face the truth?
What are those things that have a stronghold on you?

A:

Answer for yourself.

NOW LET'S WRITE
YOUR ANSWERS

Chapter 10

Saved but not Healed

On December 22, 2007, our morning started early. We were taking a road trip to Oklahoma to surprise my sister Marsha. Her son Billy died a year prior and she had started a foundation in his memory. Our children were not too thrilled about not being able to attend especially since Brittany was in town visiting from Dallas for the holidays. They were a little irritated with both of us. But, it didn't change the situation. We still left them behind making a promise that we'd return in a couple of days. Our car was packed with a change of clothing for the event. We left out pretty early trying to beat the predicted snowfall. I was all strapped in ready to go. As we traveled down the highway, we listened to music and talked about how surprised my sister would be. We had been on the road for about two and a half hours when we stopped for gas and a bathroom break at the Wichita turnpike. As I walked out of the rest stop, I looked up into the sky and saw a few snow flurries. We decided we would make it to Oklahoma, stay overnight and return the following day. We were traveling about eighty miles per hour on I-35. As we approached a curve, we noticed traffic was at a slow crawl. Moments earlier, I literally was thinking *slow this car down*. But I didn't speak up out of fear of causing an argument. The car hit black ice and sent us into a tailspin. I sat calmly in my seat as my husband wrestled with the steering wheel. I knew nothing about driving on black ice. I did know he was a well trained Major on the Kansas City police force and he had been equipped to handle a lot of difficult situations. I was completely calm about everything because I knew, without a shadow of doubt, he would not let anything happen to me. I heard him say, "Hold on, Chinda! Hold ON!" The car flipped over the embankment. As it toppled upside down hitting and hammering on the driver side, I sat calmly thinking *my husband has got this. He is proficient in his driving and he has vowed to take care of me twice.* When the car finally landed upside down, we hung there quietly. There was no sound to be heard by either of us. I was shocked that I didn't hear him cry out for me. I thought, *That is strange. He should be checking to see if I'm okay.* Somehow I managed to get out of my seat belt and reached over to check on him only to find his pulse was faint. I told him help was on the way and to hang in there. *What is going on here, Lord? Why have You allowed this to happen?* I found myself sitting on the curbside in a freezing cold winter storm WIDOWED at age 44. There I sat alone again.

I called out to God, "Lord, help ME!" I began to play what I had done over and over in my head. I knew he was in God's hands. I knew he was prepared. I knew his soul had been saved. I realized this was my life-changing event. I know an event sounds so more like a party, but it really was: *A party to salvation. A party to eternal life. A party to freedom.* He had been set free and it was my time to get it right.

I wasn't a bad person. Actually, I thought I was a rather good person. I thought I treated everyone fair. I had lots of friends who loved me. My family supported me. I had raised three beautiful children. I even had a great relationship with my father. I loved my husband and I had learned to respect him. I trusted he would supply my every need. He was the one who studied the Bible with me. He was the one who worked day and night to provide for us. He was the one who made all the decisions. When I was sad, I looked for him to make me happy. When I was sick, I trusted he would care for me. When I was hungry, he made sure our family was fed. Suddenly, I realized I had put my trust in MAN for years. When I say trust in man, that represents anything other than God first.

I heard God's voice speak clearly to me, "Do you realize that from early on you were looking for someone else to validate who you were? Do you realize that all of these years you have been looking and seeking for your father, and I have been with you all along? Think back. When you were little, who protected you from harm's way? Who provided you with shelter, clothes, and food? Who allowed a nineteen-year-old to birth a healthy baby girl? Who provided you with a strong mother to give you the foundation you needed? Who gave you siblings to love and fight with? Who gave you the strength and determination to do better? Although your dad and mom separated, I still blessed you with him. I never told you that life would be easy. I gave you my instruction manual to study and read. You haven't failed me, you failed yourself."

I had to go back and examine my heart and mind. I had to seek out counsel for my children and I. I was completely broken and clueless about how lost I was.

I made my way out of the darkness with much needed prayer and healing, searching for something once more. Not exactly knowing what that was or what it even felt like, but I knew whatever it was, it was going to be found. I had been lost for a long time. I had been presenting a facade that my life was great and everything was okay. On the outside, I looked good. I was a great mom, a good cook. I kept my house clean and went to church. I even said my prayers. I was baptized when I was in the sixth grade and rededicated my life to Christ after I had hit a few bumps in my marriage. I thanked God occasionally for all the blessings that were given to me. I can go on and on explaining how great of a person I was, but the big question was, did I really know who my Father was? Did I have a personal relationship with my Father? Did I understand the power in His name? Did I understand the Almighty had several names: Jesus, Lord, Almighty, Prince of Peace, Abba, Savior, Healer, Father, Provider, and God?

Why didn't I know when all my burdens are turned over completely to God results happen? I didn't know you couldn't rush God to do anything. And what about this jealous God? Mercy! I had neglected to have a relationship with my Heavenly Father. While I was learning everything else, why wasn't I shown the truth? The truth is, the evidence was presented to me; I just had blinders on. I didn't listen nor was I ready to receive. I was so caught up with my life.

Chapter 10

Q:

Write down the day you realized you had been saved but not healed

A:

Answer for yourself.

NOW LET'S WRITE
YOUR ANSWERS

_____

_____

_____

_____

_____

_____

_____

_____

_____

_____

_____

_____

_____

_____

_____

_____

_____

_____

_____

_____

_____

_____

_____

_____

Chapter 11

Surrender

People who loved and genuinely cared about me surrounded me with support. Sisters visited me at home and called me on the telephone offering and giving me prayer. I had begun a new journey and called it *I Surrender ALL!! All to Jesus, precious Savior, I surrender all.* As my life started to change, my thoughts became clearer. My conversation was all about the truth - the truth about my personal relationship with God, the truth about my brokenness and unhealthy relationships. I had to stop lying to myself and others about what was missing in my life and what had been keeping me in that dark space. I had to revisit some old ground, ground that was uncomfortable. I wanted and needed answers to all the questions that had manifested inside of me. God, I know you are real. You saved me once again. Lord, please turn my mess around? I don't want to be in that dark place ever again. God, I want to be able to share Your greatness with others. God, please forgive me.

God, I know you died for my sins. Lord, I repent and ask you to make me whole once again. There were many questions I needed answers to such as will I be labeled as broken and damaged by others? Will I be forgiven for all the hurt and pain I caused others? I decided whatever the cost, I was ready to release all my hurt and pain and concerns out to the universe. I was ready to meet my maker, the one who had created, shaped and molded me to be the best I could be. I confessed with my mouth and with a sincere heart. My yes to God was the beginning of a new beginning.

It's amazing what God can and will do when you are obedient to His will for your life. The fulfillment of my being was to serve others however God directed me. My commitment to understanding and learning more about the God we serve became part of my everyday life. I had something to share and to say to all who would listen and even to those who didn't want to listen. I became an advocate for Jesus Christ and telling everyone how great God is became my mission. At times, even I didn't recognize the life I had become a part of.

I boarded an aircraft with some amazing women: Lia, Shannon, and Angela. Together, we set out on a journey that none of us expected. Well, I definitely didn't expect all of its significance. We were on a mission to visit a new church plant to scope out how the structure of worship was. My friend Lia McIntosh had strategically handpicked me to be a part of something new that would transform lives forever. She later became my pastor, mentor and life coach. I had no idea my YES, the obedience I had promised to God a year prior, was about to pay off. You talking about your soul being rich and full…

When Lia asked me to be a part of her launch team, all I knew was it was no accident that she and I had connected. Lia had prayed for me during Wednesday night bible study at Hour of Power and we occasionally checked in with one another via email. One day, I made a simple telephone call to check on her and see how she was doing. Turns out, Lia was finishing up seminary and had just turned in her final paper. My call provided a much needed interruption to break up the monotony of her schoolwork. As we conversed about what was going on in our lives, there was a pause. Then, she spoke softly with great confidence and strength, "Rochinda, you know I'm getting ready to graduate from seminary and I have been appointed to start a new church in South KC." I listened quietly not thinking this had anything to do with me. I was dealing with my own stuff and I had my own plans. Lia continued saying she had been praying and asking God to send willing people to help build the Kingdom and serve others. In silence, I hung on to every word she said. Finally, she asked, "Will you journey with me?" I responded that I knew nothing about building a church. I'd never been to seminary or theology school. I couldn't quote scriptures from the Bible. The only thing I knew was my love for Christ and my experience with life after death. I had a list of everything I could not do. She responded, "I need people like you on my team with a willing heart and a yes." Eight years later here I sit, still with a yes to God for whatever He would have me to do. God is my everything.

As we entered Brown Elementary School to partake in worship with Impact Church pastored by Olu Brown, I was instructed to spend time with the hospitality team and the kid's ministry. We all were paired up with someone to guide us and answer any questions we had. We were then given a time to meet for worship. As special guests of Pastor Ol uBrown, when we made our way into worship, we were seated on the front row so we could take in everything.

I was still in disbelief. Here I was in Atlanta, Georgia, with some intelligent, smart, mighty women of God -- two of them pastors: Rev. Shannon Hancock and Rev. Lia McIntosh, and the third lady in our group, Angela Powell was just beginning seminary. All of these sisters were getting their praise on, not holding anything back. They were singing with their eyes closed, hands high in the air. It was amazing to watch them worship. I finally stood and joined in the powerful experience.

As I worshipped, I started feeling some kind of way. I felt awkward, kind of like when I was in school and the teacher had singled me out. I wanted to run and hide, but I had nowhere to go. I was trapped between Shannon on my right and Lia on my left. I tried to sit, but the music kept playing. How could I remain seated when the Holy Spirit was moving on everyone else ? Finally, I could not take it any longer. I stood to my feet, lifted my hands above my head and praised God. I wasn't sure what was happening, but I knew it was AWESOME! I jumped up and down, doing my own dance. I quickly forgot about where I was or who was with me. I didn't care who saw me. The tears flowed. I couldn't refrain myself from what I was feeling. The room was full of worshippers, but I felt so very special, like the attention I had been searching for was being given just to me. There was a bright ray of light and the presence of God was right before me. I wanted more and more of what I was feeling. I felt my body being embraced and I heard a voice telling me it was okay to release everything and turn it all over.

I had been searching for someone to take care of me for years and it was happening. God's hand was stretched out to me and I heard the voice say, "I have always been here for you in your darkest and weakest hour. When you were a little girl, I always held your hand. You were never alone. Even when you were an adolescent, I protected you and provided food and put clothing on your back. As your life progressed to being a teenager, I often appeared but you ignored me. When you became a young adult, I provided strong women around you for you to observe, but you had blinders on. When you became a wife, I gave you strict instructions on what to do, and you failed to follow. When you became a mother, I gave you three healthy babies. You needed more proof, more substance so I gave you examples. You needed something that was clear that everyone would understand. I gave you a message to share with others. I took life and spared yours. You needed a close and personal relationship with Me, I gave you new life. Now, my daughter, come and walk with Me. Come and talk to Me. I need you to trust Me with everything."

I couldn't hold back anymore. "Father God," I said, "I surrender my life over to you. Please forgive me and provide me with a clean start. God, I need you. I can't do this on my own. I am broken and I need to be made whole again." The moment I surrendered my life back over to Christ, everything began to line up in order. All this time, I had been looking and searching for an absentee father and all this time my heavenly Father had never left. My God had been keeping me for such a time as this. God, thank you for not giving up on me. Thank you for keeping me even when I didn't want to be kept.

Chapter 11

Q:

What will you surrender?

A:

Answer for yourself.

NOW LET'S WRITE
YOUR ANSWERS

_____

_____

_____

_____

_____

_____

_____

_____

_____

_____

_____

_____

_____

_____

_____

_____

_____

_____

_____

_____

_____

_____

_____

New Ground; Being Obedient

My children are all grown. My oldest daughter Brittany lives in Dallas. My son Darrell attends college at Pittsburgh State, only two and a half hours away. Baby girl Andrea is a senior in high school. I own and operate a boutique that keeps me busy. It is called *Chinda's Boutique*. The boutique was opened to connect with women and let them know there is life after death. It is a place where many come to experience deep solitude and new meaning of life. On top of that, I was part of the launch team for a new church plant and held the position of Director of Ministry. My life became so full with God's grace and mercy and the glow was evident.

I spent countless hours in deep prayer asking for needed direction to continue being pleasing to God. I no longer fit God into my schedule. I fit my schedule in with God. Listen, do not miss the significance of this. Do not think your life will ever be full or complete by giving God your leftovers. Imagine being seated at an exclusive restaurant and your server bringing you the leftovers of someone's half eaten meal. Exactly. That's how God feels when we give our leftover time. It's time to start living your best life allowing God to lead.

My passion to live my best life ever manifested and started to blossom beautifully. Being led by God took on a whole new meaning of doing and being exactly what God created me for. I am intentional about living the life God has given me. Intentional about cultivating healthy relationships with family and friends. Intentional about growing, serving and making the connections with others to live their best life ever. This new found freedom with God is amazing.

I felt like I had been given a whole new set of lenses; I can now see clearly. These lenses fit my round face perfectly and stood out in any crowd. I felt like all the darkness I had ever experienced was brought to light. I no longer walked in darkness or felt alone. I no longer looked for society to validate what was good for me. I no longer believed I wasn't deemed for greatness in all that I did. I enjoyed sharing with others about how great God is. I became an advocate for Jesus Christ. To all that will listen, I share His greatness. In the past, I had done things my way never consulting with my heavenly Father. God had my attention and I remained front and center listening and watching for directions. The directions to go left or right, up or down. Directions to say yes or no. Not maybe, not uncertainty, but a firm precise yes. God had been keeping and preserving me for this perfect timing.

The time finally came where I had the desire to marry again. I knew my heart had been healed and my past had become my memories. I spent a lot time in prayer -- early mornings, late afternoons and in the midnight hours. My prayer went something like this, "Heavenly Father, God, thank you Lord, for keeping me when I didn't want to be kept or deserved to be kept. Lord, I come to you humbly with a gracious heart with expectation of a new life with a new mate. Lord, you made me whole and you know the desires of my heart. You created me in your image, wonderfully and marvelously made. I'm asking for your direction and clarity on marrying again. If you believe I'm not ready, please sit me still. Lord, I'm READY!"

Needless to say, I was introduced to a God-fearing gentleman that loved the Lord. I hit the jackpot. I don't mean jackpot like big money, I'm talking about God's jackpot. I felt like God had pulled the lever down and out rolled blessings! The desire of my prayers were answered. Our courtship began over the telephone for about eighteen months. Our calls always began with prayer and thanking God for technology and friendship. Since my newfound love lived in Indianapolis, Indiana, this was our time to develop trust. God strategically set me up. I was set up to receive God's blessings without knowing the outcome. This was called *faith*. I learned how to communicate on a broader and deeper level. I understood what true intimacy was. God heard my cries and my whispers and concerns. I was given a relationship that taught me how to set expectations with each other. It also allowed us to get to know one another without being caught up in the physical part. Don't get me wrong, we were extremely attracted to one another but we both knew we wanted to be pleasing to our heavenly Father. I always said whatever I did in this new season, it had to be led by God only. I no longer was going to be kept by the enemy. The distance was much needed for me. I needed to show God who and where my commitment was. I was having a romance of a lifetime with my heavenly Father and was being prepared for prince charming. Glory to God! Thank you, JESUS.

I said YES! On November 22, 2014, at age fifty, Rochinda got married! How many of you believe in fairytales? As a child, we all did knowing there was a happy ending. This story definitely is a fairytale that has been directed and orchestrated by God. Each character was hand selected and created for each specific chapter. Although the story felt more like a horror story being transformed into a nightmare in the beginning, it has finally manifested into a fairytale.

When we seek God first in all that we do and wait on the answer, we will not be disappointed. I spent countless years searching and looking for someone or something to fulfill my life and make it better. What I needed was a relationship with God. I now understand what that is, someone to talk to anytime I want, who accepts me as I am without giving up on me. All of my needs have always been provided for. The love received was never with conditions. God had already experienced the pain, rejection, loss and humiliation beforehand. Who else could turn my mess into a message? God wiped my tears away and held me tight and has given me the confirmation of a proud Father telling me that I was ready.

I took my vows in front of three hundred family and friends and we all stood firm in agreement with God's love for us. All agreed to walk with us in remembrance of the love that God had joined together. I am in love with my Savior Jesus Christ who is my everything. I'm committed to following and being obedient to God's will for my life. I have been set free to experience the abundant life of freedom. I understand clearly who my Keeper is. I have been released *from being kept to being kept*!

I love life to the fullest. I have been married for two years to Sir Alan, my wonderful husband who adores me. I'm able to represent what a kept woman of God looks and acts like without any shame in my game. My children have all excelled in this new season called *life after death lead by God*. Brittany holds a Masters degree in Business and is married to a wonderful husband, Darrell Robinson. They are both proud parents of my awesome grandson, Master Jaden. My one and only son Darrell graduated from college with a Bachelors degree in Business Administration with an emphasis on Management Marketing. Baby girl Andrea earned her Bachelor of Science degree majoring in Kinesiology and is headed off to nursing school, Fall 2017.

Do not doubt what our Father can do! I said, "Won't God Do it?" I represent what a Kept Woman of God looks like!

I have been released *From Being Kept to Being Kept*

Love and Blessings,
Rochinda

Chapter 12

Q:

What does your new ground look like?
Will it be led by God?

A:

Answer for yourself.

NOW LET'S WRITE
YOUR ANSWERS

_____
_____
_____
_____
_____
_____
_____
_____
_____
_____
_____
_____
_____
_____
_____
_____
_____
_____
_____
_____
_____
_____

READING GROUP GUIDE
DISCUSSION QUESTIONS

Take your ministry/group deeper into the lessons From Being Kept to Being Kept.

1. Chapter (1) Have you ever affirmed something in your life to avoid (the truth) of something else? What helped you to confront the truth? As children, we try to make our parents proud. Have your parents ever made you proud? What was it and did you tell them you were proud? Why or Why not?
2. Did you witness detrimental habits growing up? Did you reject or adopt them in your own life? Do you find it difficult to share what you struggle with? Do you have safe spaces, people, community to share honestly with?
3. How do you define freedom? Do you have it? If not, what do you need to get rid of or do or keep doing to have it for yourself?
4. Being bullied and really uncomfortable being singled out. How do you get comfortable with being uncomfortable?
5. How many women have been brought up or taught that if a man buys you gifts or pay for things, it means he is interested in you? What are the red flags in this when he's doing this just to use or take advantage of you?
6. What are some healthy and wholesome ways a man can provide and care for you where you aren't feeling used or obligated?
7. As you read From Being Kept to Being Kept do you believe that it's important to visit your past in order to move forward? Explain why you feel it's important or not.

9. Do you believe that rejection can stifle you in moving forward? If so, how? And Why? In Chapter 4 Rochinda's recollections of being left behind by her father had a major impact on her life. What rejections will you call out and leave behind?

10. Do you believe that rejections that one receives from her father can cause one to reach for acceptance from men?

11. Why is it important to release all strongholds? How did Rochinda finally release the bondage of the world and the misconception of what she believed a Kept Woman was?

12. What was your first experience with love? Thinking back, was it real or your imagination? Do you believe that God allows us to experience heartache for comparison with the truth of God's love? Can love be measured by gifts and money? Can all these gifts cause you to stay stuck in a bad situation?

13. Chapter 11/ Why are we so scared to let go of our fears to let God take control of our lives? Once you have taken that step, how do you deal with the people who are in your life but don't know or understand that God is the way?

14. Define what a Kept Woman or Kept man of God is? What are the perks of being Kept by God? What about the Kept by the world?

15. What would be your main goal to start on after reading From Being Kept to Being Kept?

About the Author

Rochinda Pickens

Rochinda Pickens is a vessel being used by God, a loving wife, author, speaker, grandma and proud mother of three. She's a connector of women globally and has a heart for all. Rochinda's courage and determination to walk in freedom has impacted and inspired women to stand in their Truth. As Founder and Chief executive officer of Kept Woman of God, Inc. 501 (c)(3) nonprofit organization, she has helped many define their own truth and is making a difference in surrounding communities throughout the United States. Rochinda has helped developed workshops, retreats, and annual conferences that has transformed the lives of many women. She is the author of the National Best Seller, From Being Kept to Being Kept, a journey about Freedom and elevation through God's surrender. A visionary and contributing author to her book title Picking Up the Pieces. Born and raised in Kansas City, Missouri and avid philanthropist and a helper to those in need. She is a member of Sister Circle of Greater Kansas City and International Association Business Women and travels the world speaking and sharing her signature message "Walking in Freedom" Being a Kept Woman of God.

Learn more about Rochinda at www.KeptWomanofGod.com

@keptwoman0711

@keptwomanofGod   *Let's Connect!*

@keptwomanofGod

@keptwoman0711

WE WANT TO HEAR FROM YOU

If this book has made a difference in your life Rochinda would be excited to hear about it.

Please leave a review on Amazon.com

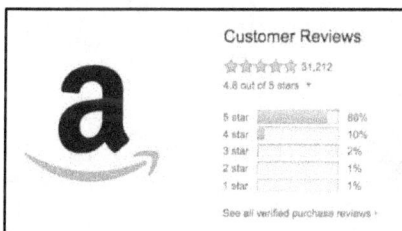

Book Rochinda to speak at your next event.
Send email to staff@KeptwomanofGod.com

ROCHINDA
PICKENS

KEPT WOMAN OF GOD MINISTRY
http://www.KeptWomanofGod.com

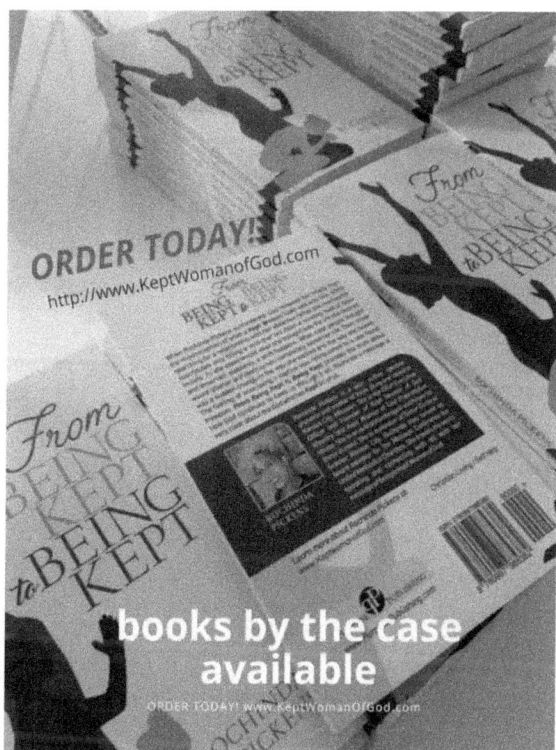

ORDER TODAY!
http://www.KeptWomanofGod.com

books by the case available

ORDER TODAY! www.KeptWomanOfGod.com

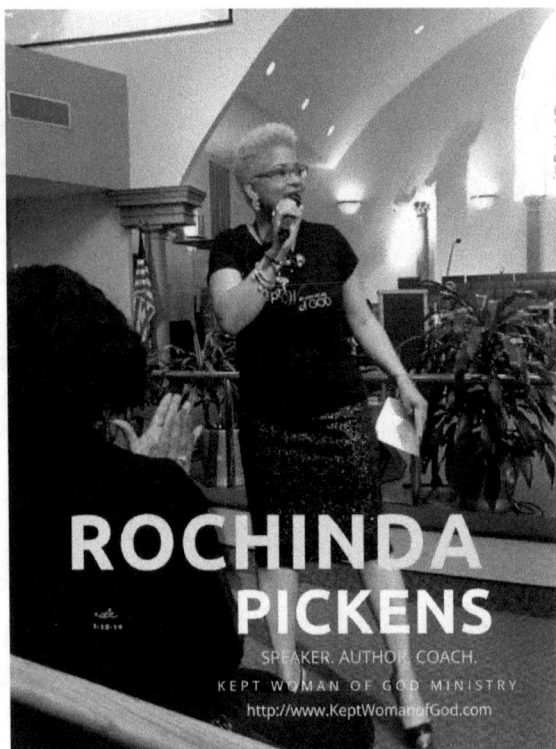

ROCHINDA
PICKENS

SPEAKER. AUTHOR. COACH.

KEPT WOMAN OF GOD MINISTRY

http://www.KeptWomanofGod.com

FREEDOM

NEED A COACH?

Hire

ROCHINDA
PICKENS

For You formed my inward parts;
You covered me in my mother's womb.
Psalm 139:13.
New King James Version (NKJV)

http://www.KeptWomanOfGod.com

KEPT WOMAN OF GOD
CONFERENCE

VOLUNTEER. EXHIBIT. SPONSOR.

While women have been given countless opportunities to connect virtually with other women from all over the world, it never quite takes the place of connecting in person-hugging the necks of sisters in Christ and sitting down to conversation over coffee.

This event is more than just a meet-and-greet - it's an immersion in the kind of love and encouragement that comes from women connecting in real life.

Join the Kept Woman of God Ministry to support women in our community.

SPEAKER. AUTHOR. COACH.

ROCHINDA PICKENS
"AND YOU WILL KNOW THE TRUTH AND THE TRUTH WILL MAKE YOU FREE." -JOHN 8:32

http://www.KeptWomanofGod.com

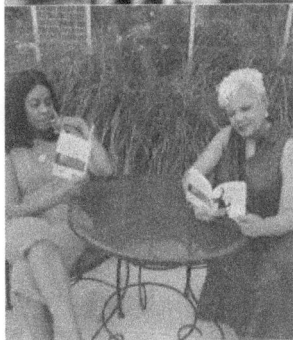

Kept Woman of GOD.

www.ingramcontent.com/pod-product-compliance
Lightning Source LLC
Chambersburg PA
CBHW052010090426
42741CB00008B/1636